HOUGHTON MIFFLIN HARCOURT

MATH Expressions
Common Core

Dr. Karen C. Fuson

GRADE

4

Volume 1

This material is based upon work supported by the
National Science Foundation
under Grant Numbers
ESI-9816320, REC-9806020, and RED-935373.

Any opinions, findings, and conclusions, or recommendations expressed in this material
are those of the author and do not necessarily reflect the views of the National Science Foundation.

HOUGHTON MIFFLIN HARCOURT

Printed in the U.S.A.

ISBN: 978-0-547-82437-6

7 8 9 10 0868 21 20 19 18 17 16 15 14

4500462239   A B C D E F G

VOLUME 1 CONTENTS

UNIT 1 Place Value and Multidigit Addition and Subtraction

© Houghton Mifflin Harcourt Publishing Company

UNIT 2 Multiplication with Whole Numbers

UNIT 4 Equations and Word Problems

STUDENT RESOURCES

Family Letter

Dear Family,

Your child is learning math in an innovative program called *Math Expressions*. In Unit 1, your child will use place value drawings and charts to understand that the value of each place is 10 times greater than the value of the place to its right. This understanding is essential when comparing, rounding, or adding multidigit numbers. *Math Expressions* encourages children to think about "making new groups" to help them understand place values.

We call the method below "New Groups Above". The numbers that represent the new groups are written above the problem.

1. Add the ones:

5 + 7 = 12 ones
12 = 2 ones + 10 ones,
and 10 ones = 1 new ten.

$$\begin{array}{r} \overset{1}{} \\ 5,1\,7\,5 \\ +\ 3,9\,6\,7 \\ \hline 2 \end{array}$$

2. Add the tens:

1 + 7 + 6 = 14 tens
14 = 4 tens + 10 tens,
and 10 tens = 1 new hundred.

$$\begin{array}{r} \overset{1\ 1}{} \\ 5,1\,7\,5 \\ +\ 3,9\,6\,7 \\ \hline 4\,2 \end{array}$$

Share with your family the Family Letter on Activity Workbook page 1.

3. Add the hundreds:

1 + 1 + 9 = 11 hundreds
11 = 1 hundred + 10 hundreds,
and 10 hundreds = 1 new thousand.

$$\begin{array}{r} \overset{1\ \ 1\ 1}{} \\ 5,1\,7\,5 \\ +\ 3,9\,6\,7 \\ \hline 1\,4\,2 \end{array}$$

4. Add the thousands:

1 + 5 + 3 = 9 thousands

$$\begin{array}{r} \overset{1\ \ 1\ 1}{} \\ 5,1\,7\,5 \\ +\ 3,9\,6\,7 \\ \hline 9,1\,4\,2 \end{array}$$

We call the following method "New Groups Below." The steps are the same, but the new groups are written below the addends.

It is easier to see the totals for each column (12 and 14) and adding is easier because you add the two numbers you see and then add the 1.

1.

$$\begin{array}{r} 5,1\,7\,5 \\ +\ 3,9\,6\,7 \\ \hline 2 \end{array}$$

2.

$$\begin{array}{r} 5,1\,7\,5 \\ +\ 3,9\,6\,7 \\ \hline 4\,2 \end{array}$$

3.

$$\begin{array}{r} 5,1\,7\,5 \\ +\ 3,9\,6\,7 \\ \hline 1\,4\,2 \end{array}$$

4.

$$\begin{array}{r} 5,1\,7\,5 \\ +\ 3,9\,6\,7 \\ \hline 9,1\,4\,2 \end{array}$$

It is important that your child maintains his or her home practice with basic multiplication and division.

Sincerely,
Your child's teacher

COMMON CORE This unit includes the Common Core Standards for Mathematical Content for Number and Operations in Base Ten and Measurement and Data, 4.NBT.1, 4.NBT.2, 4.NBT.3, 4.NBT.4, 4.MD.2 and all Mathematical Practices.

Carta a la familia

Estimada familia,

Su niño está aprendiendo matemáticas mediante el programa *Math Expressions*. En la Unidad 1, se usarán dibujos y tablas de valor posicional para comprender que el valor de cada lugar es 10 veces mayor que el valor del lugar a su derecha. Comprender esto es esencial para comparar, redondear o sumar números de varios dígitos. *Math Expressions* enseña a pensar en "formar grupos nuevos" para comprender los valores posicionales.

Este método se llama "Grupos nuevos arriba". Los números que representan los grupos nuevos se escriben arriba del problema:

Muestra a tu familia la Carta a la familia de la página 2 del Cuaderno de actividades y trabajo.

1. Suma las unidades:

$5 + 7 = 12$ unidades
$12 = 2$ unidades $+ 10$ unidades, y 10 unidades $= 1$ nueva decena.

$$\begin{array}{r} {\scriptstyle 1} \\ 5,1\,7\,5 \\ +\,3,9\,6\,7 \\ \hline 2 \end{array}$$

2. Suma las decenas:

$1 + 7 + 6 = 14$ decenas
$14 = 4$ decenas $+ 10$ decenas, y 10 decenas $= 1$ nueva centena.

$$\begin{array}{r} {\scriptstyle 1\ 1} \\ 5,1\,7\,5 \\ +\,3,9\,6\,7 \\ \hline 4\,2 \end{array}$$

3. Suma las centenas:

$1 + 1 + 9 = 11$ centenas
$11 = 1$ centenas $+ 10$ centenas, y 10 centenas $= 1$ nuevo millar.

$$\begin{array}{r} {\scriptstyle 1\ \ 1\ 1} \\ 5,1\,7\,5 \\ +\,3,9\,6\,7 \\ \hline 1\,4\,2 \end{array}$$

4. Suma los millares:

$1 + 5 + 3 = 9$ millares

$$\begin{array}{r} {\scriptstyle 1\ \ 1\ 1} \\ 5,1\,7\,5 \\ +\,3,9\,6\,7 \\ \hline 9,1\,4\,2 \end{array}$$

Este método se llama "Grupos nuevos abajo". Los pasos son iguales, pero los nuevos grupos se escriben abajo de los sumandos:

Es más fácil ver los totales de cada columna (12 y 14) y es más fácil sumar porque sumas los dos números que ves, y luego sumas 1.

1.
$$\begin{array}{r} 5,1\,7\,5 \\ +\,3,9\,6\,7 \\ \hline 2 \end{array}$$

2.
$$\begin{array}{r} 5,1\,7\,5 \\ +\,3,9\,6\,7 \\ \hline 4\,2 \end{array}$$

3.
$$\begin{array}{r} 5,1\,7\,5 \\ +\,3,9\,6\,7 \\ \hline 1\,4\,2 \end{array}$$

4.
$$\begin{array}{r} 5,1\,7\,5 \\ +\,3,9\,6\,7 \\ \hline 9,1\,4\,2 \end{array}$$

Es importante que su niño siga practicando las multiplicaciones y divisiones básicas en casa.

Atentamente,
El maestro de su niño

COMMON CORE

Esta unidad incluye los Common Core Standards for Mathematical Content for Number and Operations in Base Ten and Measurement and Data, 4.NBT.1, 4.NBT.2, 4.NBT.3, 4.NBT.4, 4.MD.2 and all Mathematical Practices.

Place Value to Thousands

► Model Hundreds

You can represent numbers by making **place value drawings** on a **dot array**.

1. What number does this drawing show?
   Explain your thinking.

► Model Thousands

Discuss this place value drawing. Write the number of each.

2. ones:

3. quick tens:

4. hundred boxes:

5. thousand bars:

6. How many hundred boxes could we draw inside each thousand bar? Explain.

7. What number does this drawing show?

▶ Model Greater Numbers

Place value can also be shown without using a dot array.

8. What number does this drawing represent?
Explain your thinking.

What would the drawing represent if it had:

9. 3 more hundred boxes?

10. 0 hundred boxes?

11. 2 fewer quick tens?

12. 2 more quick tens?

13. 0 quick tens?

14. 5 fewer ones?

15. 0 ones?

16. 4 more thousand bars?

17. On your MathBoard, make a place value drawing for a different number that has the digits 1, 2, 7, and 9.

18. Explain how your drawing is similar to and different from the drawing for 1,279.

▶ Practice with Place Value Drawings

Make a place value drawing for each number, using ones, quick tens, and hundred boxes.

19. 6

20. 3

21. 603

22. 300

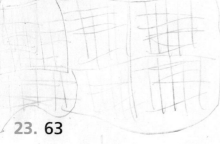

23. 63

24. 32

25. 325

26. 285

27. 109

28. 573

Class Activity

▶ **Practice Modeling Thousands**

Make a place value drawing for each number, using ones, quick tens, hundred boxes, and thousand bars.

29. 2,596

30. 3,045

6 UNIT 1 LESSON 1

Place Value to Thousands

► The Place Value Chart

Discuss the patterns you see in the Place Value Poster below.

× 10 (Greater) ←

Thousands	Hundreds	Tens	ONES
1,000.	100.	10.	1.
$\frac{1,000}{1}$	$\frac{100}{1}$	$\frac{10}{1}$	$\frac{1}{1}$
$1,000.00	$100.00	$10.00	$1

Use your Whole Number Secret Code Cards to make numbers on the frame.

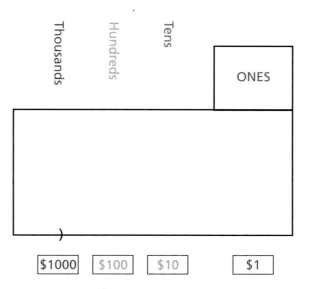

VOCABULARY
standard form
word form
expanded form

▶ Write Numbers Using Expanded Form

Standard form: 8,562

Word form: eight thousand, five hundred sixty-two

Expanded form: 8,000 + 500 + 60 + 2

Read and write each number in expanded form.

1. 73   2. 108

3. 5,621   4. 4,350

5. 8,083   6. 1,006

Read and write each number in standard form.

7. 40 + 3   8. 200 + 60 + 1

9. 900 + 5   10. 1,000 + 70 + 9

11. 5,000 + 30   12. 9,000 + 800 + 4

Read and write each number in word form.

13. 400 + 40 + 1

14. 1,000 + 50

Read and write each number in standard form.

15. thirty-five   16. three hundred five

17. six thousand, eight 18. six thousand, one hundred eight

Write the value of the underlined digit.

19. 7<u>5</u>6   20. <u>4</u>,851   21. 6,<u>5</u>07

> *Use Activity Workbook page 5.*

► Summarize Rounding Rules

Use these rounding frames as a visual aid when rounding to the nearest 10, 100, 1,000.

Nearest 10	Nearest 100	Nearest 1,000
100	1,000	10,000
90	900	9,000
80	800	8,000
70	700	7,000
60	600	6,000
50	500	5,000
40	400	4,000
30	300	3,000
20	200	2,000
10	100	1,000

Round to the nearest ten.

1. 87
2. 16
3. 171
4. 2,165
5. 5,114
6. 3,098

Round to the nearest hundred.

7. 734
8. 363
9. 178
10. 6,249
11. 8,251
12. 8,992

Round to the nearest thousand.

13. 1,275
14. 8,655
15. 5,482
16. 3,804
17. 1,501
18. 9,702

► Compare Numbers

Discuss the problem below.

Jim has 24 trading cards and Hattie has 42 trading cards.
Who has more trading cards? How do you know?

Draw a place value model for each problem.
Write > (greater than), < (less than), or = to make
each statement true.

19. 26 ⬤ 29   20. 44 ⬤ 34   21. 26 ⬤ 62

Compare using >, <, or =.

22. 74 ⬤ 77   23. 85 ⬤ 58   24. 126 ⬤ 162

25. 253 ⬤ 235   26. 620 ⬤ 602   27. 825 ⬤ 528

28. 478 ⬤ 488   29. 3,294 ⬤ 3,924   30. 8,925 ⬤ 9,825

31. 6,706 ⬤ 6,760   32. 4,106 ⬤ 4,016   33. 1,997 ⬤ 1,799

34. 9,172 ⬤ 9,712   35. 5,296 ⬤ 5,269   36. 7,684 ⬤ 7,684

▶ Discuss and Summarize

Use Activity Workbook page 6.

Patterns to Millions

Hundred Millions	Ten Millions	Millions	Hundred Thousands	Ten Thousands	Thousands	Hundreds	Tens	Ones
100,000,000	10,000,000	1,000,000	100,000	10,000	1,000	100	10	1
millions			*thousands*			*[ones]*		

The Patterns to Millions chart shows that each digit in the number has a place value name. When we read a number, we do not say the place value name. We say the group name.

We say the word *million* after the digits in the millions group.

We say the word *thousand* after the digits in the thousands group.

We do not say the word *ones* after the digits in the ones group.

To read greater numbers, say each group of digits as if they were in the hundreds, tens, and ones places and then add the special name for that group.

▶ Read Numbers

Use your Whole Number Secret Code cards to make the groups of digits as shown below. Put them in the spaces on the Reading Millions Frame below to read them.

| 28,374 | 123,456 | 458,726 | 654,321 | 92,148 | 789,321 |

Reading Millions Frame

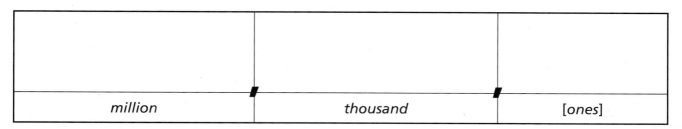

| *million* | *thousand* | *[ones]* |

▶ Read and Write Expanded Form

Read and write each number in expanded form.

1. 32,568

2. 820,149

3. 405,763

4. 703,070

Read and write each number in standard form.

5. 20,000 + 4,000 + 800 + 10 + 7

6. 700,000 + 50,000 + 3,000 + 200 + 90 + 6

7. 300,000 + 3,000 + 10 + 9

8. 800,000 + 40,000 + 400 + 80

Read and write each number in word form.

9. 90,000 + 7,000 + 300 + 20 + 4

10. 600,000 + 30,000 + 4,000 + 700 + 30

11. 200,000 + 3,000 + 80 + 6

12. 500,000 + 20,000 + 400 + 1

Read and write each number in standard form.

13. seventy-eight thousand, one hundred five

14. one million

15. five hundred sixty-three thousand, fifty-two

► Compare Greater Numbers

Discuss the problem below.

A stadium hosted both a concert and a sporting event. The concert had 101,835 people in attendance. The sporting event had 101,538 people in attendance. Which event had more people in attendance? How do you know?

Compare. Write >, <, or = to make each statement true.

1. 12,563 ⬤ 11,987

2. 14,615 ⬤ 15,651

3. 23,487 ⬤ 28,734

4. 83,342 ⬤ 80,423

5. 79,131 ⬤ 79,113

6. 126,348 ⬤ 162,634

7. 705,126 ⬤ 705,126

8. 532,834 ⬤ 532,843

9. 647,313 ⬤ 647,310

10. 198,593 ⬤ 98,593

11. 75,621 ⬤ 705,126

12. 1,000,000 ⬤ 100,000

► Greatest Place Value

Round to the nearest ten thousand.

13. 25,987

14. 13,738

15. 48,333

16. 84,562

17. 92,132

18. 99,141

Round to the nearest hundred thousand.

19. 531,987

20. 701,828

21. 670,019

22. 249,845

23. 390,101

24. 999,999

▶ **Round to Any Place**

Show your work on your paper or in your journal.

Solve.

25. A number, containing no zeros, changed to 310,000 after it was rounded. To what place was the number rounded? Explain how you know.

26. A number, containing no zeros, changed to 901,400 after it was rounded. To what place was the number rounded? Explain how you know.

27. A number, containing no zeros, changed to 800,000 after it was rounded. To what place was the number rounded? Explain how you know.

28. A number, containing no zeros, changed to 122,000 after it was rounded. To what place was the number rounded? Explain how you know.

29. What is 395,101 rounded to the nearest: ⌐

    a. ten?

    b. hundred?

    c. thousand?

    d. ten thousand?

    e. hundred thousand?

30. What is 958,069 rounded to the nearest:

    a. ten?

    b. hundred?

    c. thousand?

    d. ten thousand?

    e. hundred thousand?

Compare and Round Greater Numbers

► Discuss Different Methods

Discuss how each addition method can be used to add 4-digit numbers.

5,879 + 6,754

1. New Groups Above Method

Step 1	Step 2	Step 3	Step 4
¹	¹ ¹	¹ ¹¹	¹ ¹¹
5,879	5,879	5,879	5,879
+ 6,754	+ 6,754	+ 6,754	+ 6,754
3	33	633	12,633

2. New Groups Below Method

Step 1	Step 2	Step 3	Step 4
5,879	5,879	5,879	5,879
+ 6,754	+ 6,754	+ 6,754	+ 6,754
3	33	633	12,633

3. Show Subtotals Method (Right-to-Left)

Step 1	Step 2	Step 3	Step 4	Step 5
5,879	5,879	5,879	5,879	5,879
+ 6,754	+ 6,754	+ 6,754	+ 6,754	+ 6,754
13	13	13	13	**13**
	120	120	120	**120**
		1,500	1,500	**1,500**
			11,000	+ **11,000**
				12,633

► PATH to FLUENCY Practice

4.	5.	6.	7.
908	692	5,362	3,786
+ 653	+ 543	+ 3,746	+ 6,335

► PATH to FLUENCY **Practice (continued)**

8.	2,782	9.	6,293	10.	3,729	11.	8,196
	+ 5,246		+ 3,862		+ 4,541		+ 3,865

12.	7,862	13.	2,764	14.	4,825	15.	5,364
	+ 2,839		+ 6,648		+ 2,467		+ 4,754

► **Addition and Money**

Think about how to solve this problem.

Carlos is saving money to buy a skateboard. He saved $27 one week and $14 the next week. How much did Carlos save altogether?

Solve each problem.

16. Robyn's grandmother gave her $38 for her birthday and her uncle gave her $25. How much did Robyn get altogether?

17. A parent-teacher club sold baked goods to raise money for the school. They collected $268 on Friday and $479 on Saturday. How much did they collect altogether?

► # Analyze Different Methods

New Groups Above

Step 1	Step 2	Step 3	Step 4	Step 5	Step 6
273,608 + 591,729 7	¹ 273,608 + 591,729 37	¹ ¹ 273,608 + 591,729 337	¹ 273,608 + 591,729 5,337	¹ ¹ 273,608 + 591,729 65,337	¹ ¹ ¹ 273,608 + 591,729 865,337

New Groups Below

Step 1	Step 2	Step 3	Step 4	Step 5	Step 6
273,608 + 591,729 7	273,608 + 591,729 ₁ 37	273,608 + 591,729 ₁₁ 337	273,608 + 591,729 ₁ 5,337	273,608 + 591,729 ₁₁ 65,337	273,608 + 591,729 ₁₁₁ 865,337

Show Subtotals (Left-to-Right)

Step 1	Step 2	Step 3	Step 4	Step 5	Step 6	Step 7
273,608 + 591,729 700,000	273,608 + 591,729 700,000 160,000	273,608 + 591,729 700,000 160,000 4,000	273,608 + 591,729 700,000 160,000 4,000 1,300	273,608 + 591,729 700,000 160,000 4,000 1,300 20	273,608 + 591,729 700,000 160,000 4,000 1,300 20 17	273,608 + 591,729 700,000 160,000 4,000 1,300 20 + 17 865,337

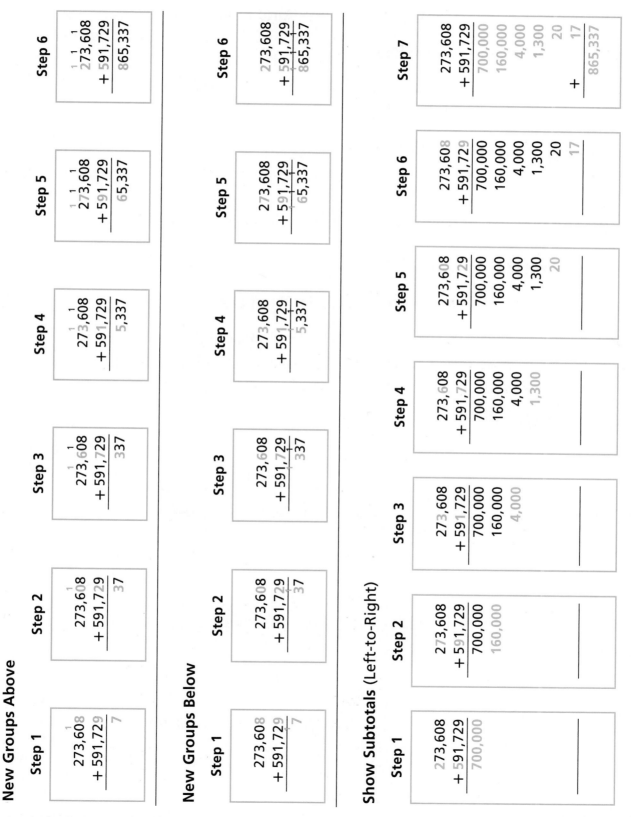

► Find the Mistake

When you add, it is important that you add **digits** in like places.

Look at the these addition exercises.

$43,629 + 5,807$ $1,468 + 327,509$ $470,952 + 4,306$

$$
\begin{array}{r}
43,629 \\
+\ 5,807 \\
\hline
101,699
\end{array}
\qquad
\begin{array}{r}
1,468 \\
+\ 327,509 \\
\hline
474,309
\end{array}
\qquad
\begin{array}{r}
470,952 \\
+\ 4,306 \\
\hline
901,552
\end{array}
$$

1. Discuss the mistake that appears in all three exercises above.

► PATH to FLUENCY Practice Aligning Places

Copy each exercise, aligning places correctly. Then add.

2. $2,647 + 38$ **3.** $156 + 83,291$

4. $4,389 + 49,706$ **5.** $135,826 + 2,927$

6. $347,092 + 6,739$ **7.** $15,231 + 697,084$

8. Write an addition word problem that has an answer
   of $43,568.

▶ Use Estimation

You can use rounding to estimate a total. Then you can adjust your estimated total to find the exact total.

The best-selling fruits at Joy's Fruit Shack are peaches and bananas. During one month Joy sold 397 peaches and 412 bananas.

1. *About* how many peaches and bananas did she sell in all?

2. *Exactly* how many peaches and bananas did she sell?

Estimate. Then adjust your estimate to find the exact answer.

3. $89 + 28$

4. $153 + 98$

5. $1,297 + 802$

6. $1,066 + 45,104$

Solve.

Tomás has $100. He wants to buy a $38 camera. He also wants to buy a $49 CD player and 2 CDs that are on sale 2 for $8.

7. How can Tomás figure out whether he has enough money for all four items? Does he have enough?

▶ Use Estimation (continued)

Solve.

Students at Washington Middle School collected 1,598 cans during the first month of their aluminum drive. During the second month of the drive, they collected 2,006 cans.

8. About how many cans did the students collect in all?

9. Exactly how many cans did the students collect in all?

▶ Look for "Easy" Combinations

You can sometimes find number combinations that make it possible to add numbers mentally.

10. Add 243, 274, 252, and 231 vertically.

11. Explain how you can use number combinations to help you add the numbers.

▶ Share Solutions

Find the total. Add mentally if you can.

12.	8	13.	46	14.	35	15.	348	16.	147
	4		21		29		516		182
	6		+ 64		75		+ 492		108
	+ 2				+ 61				+ 165

Dear Family,

Your child is now learning about subtraction. A common subtraction mistake is subtracting in the wrong direction. Children may think that they always subtract the smaller digit from the larger digit, but this is not true. To help children avoid this mistake, the *Math Expressions* program encourages children to "fix" numbers first and then subtract.

$$\begin{array}{r} 1,6\cancel{3}4 \\ -\ \cancel{1}58 \\ \hline 1,5\cancel{2}4 \end{array}$$

When one or more digits in the top number are smaller than the corresponding digits in the bottom number, fix the numbers by "ungrouping." For example, $1,634 - 158$ is shown below:

1. We cannot subtract 8 ones from 4 ones. We get more ones by ungrouping 1 ten to make 10 ones.

We now have 14 ones and only 2 tens.

$$\begin{array}{r} {}^{2\ 14}\\ 1,6\,\cancel{3}\,\cancel{4} \\ -\ 1\ 5\ 8 \end{array}$$

2. We cannot subtract 5 tens from 2 tens. We get more tens by ungrouping 1 hundred to make 10 tens.

We now have 12 tens and only 5 hundreds.

$$\begin{array}{r} {}^{12}\\ 5\ \cancel{2}\,14\\ 1,\cancel{6}\,\cancel{3}\,\cancel{4} \\ -\ 1\ 5\ 8 \end{array}$$

3. Now we can subtract:
$1 - 0 = 1$ thousand
$5 - 1 = 4$ hundreds
$12 - 5 = 7$ tens
$14 - 8 = 6$ ones

$$\begin{array}{r} {}^{12}\\ 5\ \cancel{2}\,14\\ 1,\cancel{6}\,\cancel{3}\,\cancel{4} \\ -\ 1\ 5\ 8 \\ \hline 1,4\ 7\ 6 \end{array}$$

> Share with your family the Family Letter on Activity Workbook page 7.

In the method above, the numbers are ungrouped from right to left, but students can also ungroup from left to right. Children can choose whichever way works best for them.

Your child should also continue to practice multiplication and division skills at home.

If you have any questions or comments, please call or write me.

Sincerely,
Your child's teacher

COMMON CORE This unit includes the Common Core Standards for Mathematical Content for Number and Operations in Base Ten and Measurement and Data 4.NBT.3, 4.NBT.4, 4.MD.2 and all Mathematical Practices.

Estimada familia:

Ahora su niño está aprendiendo a restar. Un error muy común al restar, es hacerlo en la dirección equivocada. Los niños pueden pensar que siempre se resta el dígito más pequeño del dígito más grande, pero no es verdad. Para ayudar a los niños a no cometer este error, el programa *Math Expressions* les propone "arreglar" los números primero y luego restar.

$$\begin{array}{r} \cancel{1,634} \\ -\ \cancel{158} \\ \hline \cancel{1,524} \end{array}$$

Cuando uno o más dígitos del número de arriba son más pequeños que los dígitos correspondientes del número de abajo, se arreglan los números "desagrupándolos". Por ejemplo, $1,634 - 158$ se muestra abajo:

Muestra a tu familia la Carta a la familia de la página 8 del Cuaderno de actividades y trabajo.

1. No podemos restar 8 unidades de 4 unidades. Obtenemos más unidades al desagrupar 1 decena para formar 10 unidades.

Ahora tenemos 14 unidades y solamente 2 decenas.

$$\begin{array}{r} {\scriptstyle 2\,14} \\ 1,6\,\cancel{3}\,\cancel{4} \\ -\ 158 \\ \hline \end{array}$$

2. No podemos restar 5 decenas de 2 decenas. Obtenemos más decenas al desagrupar 1 centena para formar 10 decenas.

Ahora tenemos 12 decenas y solamente 5 centenas.

$$\begin{array}{r} {\scriptstyle 12} \\ {\scriptstyle 5\,\cancel{2}14} \\ 1,\cancel{6}\,\cancel{3}\,\cancel{4} \\ -\ 158 \\ \hline \end{array}$$

3. Ahora podemos restar:
$1 - 0 = 1$ millar
$5 - 1 = 4$ centenas
$12 - 5 = 7$ decenas
$14 - 8 = 6$ unidades

$$\begin{array}{r} {\scriptstyle 12} \\ {\scriptstyle 5\,\cancel{2}14} \\ 1,\cancel{6}\,\cancel{3}\,\cancel{4} \\ -\ 158 \\ \hline 1,476 \end{array}$$

En el método de arriba se desagrupan los números de derecha a izquierda, pero también se pueden desagrupar de izquierda a derecha. Los niños pueden escoger la manera que les resulte más fácil.

Su niño también debe seguir practicando las destrezas de multiplicación y de división en casa.

Si tiene alguna pregunta, por favor comuníquese conmigo.

Atentamente,
El maestro de su niño

COMMON CORE Esta unidad incluye los Common Core Standards for Mathematical Content for Number and Operations in Base Ten and Measurement and Data 4.NBT.3, 4.NBT.4, 4.MD.2 and all Mathematical Practices.

▶ Discuss Ungrouping With Zeros

Look inside the magnifying glass and discuss each ungrouping step.

1. Ungroup step-by-step: *or*

2. Ungroup all at once:

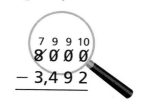

▶ Decide When to Ungroup

3. Ungroup left-to-right: *or*

4. Ungroup right-to-left:

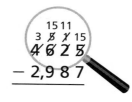

▶ Other Ungrouping Situations

5. When we have zeros and other digits on the top:

6. When we have the same digit on the top and bottom:

▶  Practice

Subtract. Show your new groups.

7.   634
   − 256

8.   800
   − 691

9.   9,462
   − 5,678

Subtract. Show your new groups.

Use Activity Workbook page 9.

10.	7,919	11.	8,502	12.	4,221
	− 3,846		− 3,749		− 2,805

13.	7,000	14.	4,650	15.	4,605
	− 572		− 2,793		− 1,711

16.	3,120	17.	6,082	18.	2,107
	− 38		− 95		− 428

19.	1,852	20.	3,692	21.	8,715
	− 964		− 2,704		− 6,742

22.	6,000	23.	7,400	24.	3,583
	− 4,351		− 1,215		− 1,794

Solve.

25. Jake has 647 pennies in his penny collection album. The album has space for 1,000 pennies. How many more pennies can Jake place in his album?

26. A ship is making an 8,509-mile voyage. So far, it has sailed 2,957 miles. How many miles of the voyage remain?

▶ Relate Addition to Subtraction

Addition and subtraction are **inverse operations**.
Break-apart drawings help to show inverse relationships.

1. Write a word problem that requires adding 1,310 and 2,057.

Show your work on your paper or in your journal.

2. Write the **addends** and the sum in the break-apart drawing.

3. Complete the two addition problems represented by the break-apart drawing.

$$
\begin{array}{r}
1{,}310 \\
+ \quad\rule{0.6cm}{0.35cm} \\
\hline
3{,}367
\end{array}
\qquad
\begin{array}{r}
2{,}057 \\
+ \quad\rule{0.6cm}{0.35cm} \\
\hline
\rule{0.6cm}{0.35cm}
\end{array}
$$

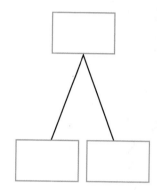

4. Write a word problem that requires subtracting 1,310 from 3,367.

5. Write two subtraction problems represented by the break-apart drawing.

Show your work on your paper or in your journal.

▶ **PATH to FLUENCY Practice**

**Subtract. Then use addition to check the subtraction.
Show your work.**

6. 1,900
   − 574
   _____

    Check:

7. 1,800
   − 1,216
   _____

    Check:

8. 5,192
   − 341
   _____

    Check:

9. 6,350
   − 2,460
   _____

    Check:

10. 7,523
    − 3,424
    _____

     Check:

11. 2,000
    − 651
    _____

     Check:

Solve.

12. In April, the zookeepers fed the penguins 4,620 fish.
    In May, they fed the penguins 5,068 fish. How many
    fish did they feed the penguins altogether?

13. The head keeper knew how many fish the penguins
    had been fed altogether, and she knew they had been
    fed 4,620 fish in April. Write a subtraction problem to
    show how the keeper could determine the number of
    fish the penguins had been fed in May.

► Find and Correct Mistakes

Always check your work. Many mistakes can be easily fixed.

What is the mistake in each problem? How can you fix the mistake and find the correct answer?

1. 67,308 − 5,497

```
         12
       6 13 10
      6 7 3 0 8
    −   5,4 9 7
    ─────────────
      1 2,3 3 8
```

2. 134,865 − 5,294

```
      1 3 4,8 6 5
    −       5,2 9 4
    ─────────────────
      1 3 1,6 3 1
```

► Check Subtraction by "Adding Up"

"Add up" to find any places where there is a subtraction mistake. Discuss how each mistake might have been made and correct the subtraction if necessary.

3.	4.	5.	6.
163,406	526,741	1,000,000	5,472,639
− 84,357	− 139,268	− 300,128	− 2,375,841
79,159	413,473	600,872	3,096,798

7. Write and solve a subtraction problem with numbers in the hundred thousands.

Show your work on your paper or in your journal.

▶ Estimate Differences

You can use estimation to decide if an answer is reasonable.

$8,000 - 6,000 = 2,000$

Dan did this subtraction: 8,196 − 5,980. His answer was 3,816. Discuss how using estimation can help you decide if his answer is correct.

Decide whether each answer is reasonable. Show your estimate.

4,000 − 5,000   1,000
                  900

8. 4,914 − 949 = 3,065

$5,000 - 900 = 4,100$

9. 52,022 − 29,571 = 22,451

Solve.

10. Bob has 3,226 marbles in his collection. Mia has 1,867 marbles. Bob says he has 2,359 more than Mia. Is Bob's answer reasonable? Show your estimate.

11. Two towns have populations of 24,990 and 12,205. Gretchen says the difference is 12,785. Is Gretchen's answer reasonable? Show your estimate.

12. Estimate to decide if the answer is reasonable. If it is not reasonable, describe the mistake and find the correct answer.

$$\begin{array}{r} 805,716 \\ - 290,905 \\ \hline 614,811 \end{array}$$

Subtract Greater Numbers

▶ Discuss the Steps of the Problem

Sometimes you will need to work through more than one step to solve a problem. The steps can be shown in one or more equations.

1. In the morning, 19 students were working on a science project. In the afternoon, 3 students left and 7 more students came to work on the project. How many students were working on the project at the end of the day?

2. Solve the problem again by finishing Anita's and Chad's methods. Then discuss what is alike and what is different about each method.

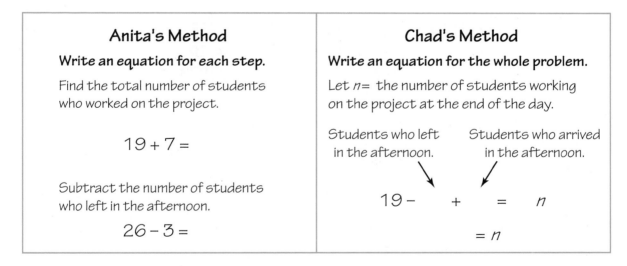

Anita's Method	Chad's Method
Write an equation for each step.	**Write an equation for the whole problem.**
Find the total number of students who worked on the project.	Let $n=$ the number of students working on the project at the end of the day.
$19 + 7 =$	Students who left in the afternoon. Students who arrived in the afternoon.
Subtract the number of students who left in the afternoon.	$19 - \quad + \quad = \quad n$
$26 - 3 =$	$= n$

3. Solve. Discuss the steps you used.

A team is scheduled to play 12 games. Of those games, 7 will be played at home. The other games are away games. How many fewer away games than home games will be played?

▶ Share Solutions

Solve each problem.

4. The school library has 288 science books. Altogether the library has 618 science and animal books. How many fewer science books than animal books does the library have?

5. Olivia's stamp collection consists of 442 stamps. There are 131 butterfly stamps and 107 dolphin stamps in her collection. How many of Olivia's stamps are not of butterflies or dolphins?

▶ PATH to FLUENCY Practice Multidigit Addition and Subtraction

6. 985
  − 792

7. 2,931
  + 8,563

8. 4,201
  + 9,979

9. 98,309
  − 48,659

10. 78,196
  − 14,587

11. 21,682
  + 95,436

12. 373,095
  + 185,543

13. 709,032
  − 239,125

14. 540,721
  + 375,699

Show your work on your paper or in your journal.

▶ Discuss Problem Types

Think different types of problems for each exercise.
Write an equation for the problem then solve it.

1. $a + 278 = 747$

747
/   \
a   278

2. $b - 346 = 587$

b
/   \
346   587

3.

933
/   \
c   346

4.

747
e   469

▶ PATH to FLUENCY Share Solutions

Write an equation for the problem then solve it.
Make a math drawing if you need to.

5. Of 800,000 species of insects, about 560,000 undergo complete metamorphosis. How many species do not undergo complete metamorphosis?

6. The Great Pyramid of Giza has about 2,000,000 stone blocks. A replica has 1,900,000 fewer blocks. How many blocks are in the replica?

7. Last year 439,508 people visited Fun Town. This is 46,739 fewer visitors than this year. How many people visited Fun Town this year?

Show your work on your paper or in your journal.

▶ PATH to FLUENCY **Share Solutions (continued)**

8. At the end of a baseball game, there were 35,602 people in the stadium. There were 37,614 people in the stadium at the beginning of the game. How many people left before the game ended?

9. This year Pinnacle Publishing printed 64,924 more books than Premier Publishing. If Pinnacle printed 231,069 books, how many books did Premier print?

10. Mary drove her car 2,483 miles during a road trip. Now she has 86,445 miles on her car. How many miles did her car have before her trip?

11. The Elbe River in Europe is 1,170 km long. The Yellow River in China is 5,465 km long. How long are the two rivers altogether?

12. A bridge is 1,595 feet long. Each cable holding up the bridge is 1,983 feet longer than the bridge itself. How long is each cable?

Problem Solving With Greater Numbers

▶ Subtraction and Money

Sondra had $140 to spend on new clothes for school. She bought a shirt for $21. You can use a model to help you find out how much money she has left.

Sondra had _____ left.

Solve each problem. Use money if you need to.

13. Jason had $30. He gave $18 to his brother. How much money does Jason have left?

14. Elana's coach had some money to spend on softball equipment. She spent $76 on bases. She has $174 left. How much did she have to start?

15. The school science club raised $325. After buying equipment for an experiment they had $168 left. How much did they spend?

16. Amy paid $575 for new furniture. Before buying it she had $813. How much did she have afterward?

Show your work on your paper or in your journal.

► **Determine Reasonable Answers**

Solve each problem. Check your answers using inverse operations.

17. Mrs. Washington has $265. She wants to by shoes for $67 and dresses for $184. Does she have enough money? Explain your answer.

18. Terrell wants to run a total of 105 miles during the month. He ran a total of 87 miles during the first 3 weeks of the month. How much does he have to run on the 4th week to make his goal?

► **What's the Error?**

Dear Math Students,

My friend is taking a trip to Antarctica. He gave me $112 to buy him some clothes. I tried to buy a parka and two pairs of wool socks, but the clerk said I didn't have enough money. I added up the cost like this:

$98 + $12 = $110

Can you help me figure out what I did wrong?

Your friend,
Puzzled Penguin

Bill's Outdoor Wear

Pair of Wool socks	$12
Hat	$15
Mitten	$10
Parka	$98

19. Write a response to Puzzled Penguin.

1-14
Class Activity

Use Activity
Workbook page 10.

► Math and Bridges

Bridges are structures that are built
to get over obstacles like water,
a valley, or roads. Bridges can be
made of concrete, steel, or even
tree roots. Engineers and designers
do a lot of math to be sure a bridge
will stand up to its use and the
forces of nature that affect it.

Lengths of Bridges		
Bridge	Length Over Water (ft)	
Manchac Swamp Bridge, U.S.A.	121,440	
Hangzhou Bay Bridge, China	117,057	
Lake Pontchartrain Causeway, U.S.A.	125,664	
Jiaozhou Bay Bridge, China	139,392	

1. Use the data in the table above to make a bar graph.

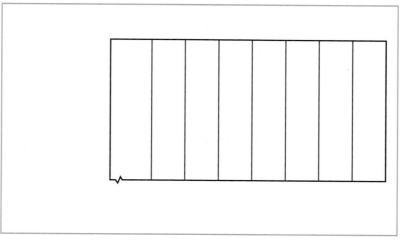

• Image Credits: ©Felipe Gabaldon/Getty Images

Show your work
on your paper or
in your journal.

▶ Add and Subtract Greater Numbers

Lake Pontchartrain Causeway, U.S.A

For Exercises 2–5, use the data in the table on Student Book page 35.

2. How much longer is the Lake Pontchartrain Causeway than the Hangzhou Bay Bridge?

3. What is the difference in length between the longest bridge and shortest bridge listed in the table?

4. Liang's goal is to ride over the Hangzhou Bay Bridge and the Jiaozhou Bay Bridge. Tanya wants to ride over the Lake Pontchartrain Causeway and the Manchac Swamp Bridge. Who will travel the greater distance on the bridges? How many more feet will he or she travel?

5. The Danyang-Kunshan Grand Bridge in China is the longest bridge over land and water in the world. It is 401,308 feet longer than the Jiaozhou Bay Bridge. How long is the Danyan-Kunshan Grand Bridge?

• Image Credits: ©David Frazier/Corbis

Focus on Mathematical Practices

Use the Activity Workbook Unit Test on pages 11–12.

► **Vocabulary**

Choose the best term from the box.

1. Addition and subtraction are _____ because one operation undoes the other. (Lesson 1-10)

2. 3,957 and 4,218 are the _____ in the problem 3,957 + 4,218. (Lessons 1-11, 1-13)

► **Concepts and Skills**

3. Use expanded form to explain how the value of the digit 4 in the number 4,444 changes for each place value. (Lesson 1-2)

4. Which is greater, the value of the digit 6 in 650 or the value of the digit 6 in 760? Explain. (Lesson 1-2)

5. Which of these numbers has the digit 7 with a value of 700: 7,352, 720, 270, 357? Explain. (Lesson 1-2)

Read and write the number in another form. (Lesson 1-4)

6. 453,208 in word form:

7. ninety thousand, thirty-three in standard form:

8. 680,742 in expanded form

Compare using >, <, or =. (Lesson 1-3, 1-5)

9. 84,055 ● 84,505   10. 7,862 ● 7,826   11. 369,125 ● 396,124

Round each number to the place value of the underlined digit.
(Lesson 1-3, 1-5)

12. 3<u>3</u>,875

13. <u>9</u>20,812

Add or subtract. (Lessons 1-6, 1-7, 1-9, 1-10, 1-11, 1-12)

14.　　1,472
　　+ 5,178

15.　　58,290
　　− 31,602

16.　　483,958
　　+ 126,081

17.　　795,236
　　− 478,517

► Problem Solving

Solve.

18. There were 3,982 people at the soccer game on Thursday. There were 1,886 more people at the soccer game on Saturday. How many people in all attended both games? (Lessons 1-6, 1-12)

19. One machine makes 125,200 small paper clips in one day. Another machine makes 83,650 large paper clips in one day. How many fewer large paper clips than small paper clips are made in one day? (Lessons 1-11, 1-12, 1-13)

20. **Extended Response** Determine whether the following statement is true or false. Explain your thinking. (Lessons 1-6, 1-9, 1-10)

$$6,421 - (284 + 653) = (6,421 - 284) + 653$$

Family Letter

Dear Family,

In this unit, your child will be learning about the common multiplication method that most adults know. However, they will also explore ways to draw multiplication. *Math Expressions* uses area of rectangles to show multiplication.

	30	+	7
20	20 × 30 = 600		20 × 7 = 140
+			
4	4 × 30 = 120		4 × 7 = 28

Area Method:

$20 \times 30 = 600$
$20 \times 7 = 140$
$4 \times 30 = 120$
$\underline{4 \times 7 = 28}$
Total = 888

Shortcut Method:

$$\begin{array}{r} \overset{1}{}\overset{2}{} \\ 37 \\ \times\ 24 \\ \hline 148 \\ 74 \\ \hline 888 \end{array}$$

Area drawings help all students see multiplication. They also help students remember what numbers they need to multiply and what numbers make up the total.

Your child will also learn to find products involving single-digit numbers, tens, and hundreds by factoring the tens or hundreds. For example,

$$200 \times 30 = 2 \times 100 \times 3 \times 10$$
$$= 2 \times 3 \times 100 \times 10$$
$$= 6 \times 1{,}000 = 6{,}000$$

By observing the zeros patterns in products like these, your child will learn to do such multiplications mentally.

If your child is still not confident with single-digit multiplication and division, we urge you to set aside a few minutes every night for multiplication and division practice. In a few more weeks, the class will be doing multidigit division, so it is very important that your child be both fast and accurate with basic multiplication and division.

If you need practice materials, please contact me.

Sincerely,
Your child's teacher

Share with your family the Family Letter on Activity Workbook page 13.

 COMMON CORE

This unit includes the Common Core Standards for Mathematical Content for Operations and Algebraic Thinking, Number and Operations in Base Ten and Measurement and Data, 4.OA.3, 4.NBT.1, 4.NBT.2, 4.NBT.3, 4.NBT.5, 4.MD.2 and all Mathematical Practices.

Carta a la familia

Estimada familia:

En esta unidad, su niño estará aprendiendo el método de multiplicación común que la mayoría de los adultos conoce. Sin embargo, también explorará maneras de dibujar la multiplicación. Para mostrar la multiplicación, *Math Expressions* usa el método del área del rectángulo.

Muestra a tu familia la Carta a la familia de la página 14 del Cuaderno de actividades y trabajo.

	30	+	7
20	$20 \times 30 = 600$		$20 \times 7 = 140$
+			
4	$4 \times 30 = 120$		$4 \times 7 = 28$

Método del área

$20 \times 30 = 600$
$20 \times 7 = 140$
$4 \times 30 = 120$
$\underline{4 \times 7 = 28}$
Total $= 888$

Método más corto

$$\begin{array}{r} \overset{1}{\underset{2}{}} \\ 37 \\ \times\,24 \\ \hline 148 \\ 74 \\ \hline 888 \end{array}$$

Los dibujos de área ayudan a los estudiantes a visualizar la multiplicación. También los ayuda a recordar cuáles números tienen que multiplicar y cuáles números forman el total.

Su niño también aprenderá a hallar productos relacionados con números de un solo dígito, con decenas y con centenas, factorizando las decenas o las centenas. Por ejemplo:

$$200 \times 30 = 2 \times 100 \times 3 \times 10$$
$$= 2 \times 3 \times 100 \times 10$$
$$= 6 \times 1{,}000 = 6{,}000$$

Al observar los patrones de ceros en productos como estos, su niño aprenderá a hacer dichas multiplicaciones mentalmente.

Si su niño todavía no domina la multiplicación y la división con números de un solo dígito, le sugerimos que dedique algunos minutos todas las noches para practicar la multiplicación y la división. Dentro de pocas semanas, la clase hará divisiones con números de varios dígitos, por eso es muy importante que su niño haga las operaciones básicas de multiplicación y de división de manera rápida y exacta.

Si necesita materiales para practicar, comuníquese conmigo.

Atentamente,
El maestro de su niño

COMMON CORE

Esta unidad incluye los Common Core Standards for Mathematical Content for Operations and Algebraic Thinking, Number and Operations in Base Ten and Measurement and Data, 4.OA.3, 4.NBT.1, 4.NBT.2, 4.NBT.3, 4.NBT.5, 4.MD.2 and all Mathematical Practices.

Arrays and Area Models

VOCABULARY
array
area

▶ Model a Product of Ones

The number of unit squares in an **array** of connected unit squares is the **area** of the rectangle formed by the squares. We sometimes just show the measurement of length and width.

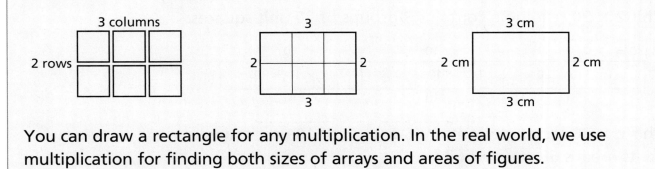

You can draw a rectangle for any multiplication. In the real world, we use multiplication for finding both sizes of arrays and areas of figures.

A 2 × 3 rectangle has 6 unit squares inside, so 2 × 3 = 6.

1. On your MathBoard, draw a 3 × 2 rectangle. How is the 3 × 2 rectangle similar to the 2 × 3 rectangle? How is it different?

2. How do the areas of the 2 × 3 and 3 × 2 rectangles compare?

VOCABULARY
square units

▶ Factor the Tens to Multiply Ones and Tens

This 2 × 30 rectangle contains 2 groups of 30 unit squares.

$$
\begin{array}{c}
30 \\
\begin{array}{|c|}
\hline
1 \times 30 = 30 \\
\hline
1 \times 30 = 30 \\
\hline
\end{array} \\
30
\end{array}
$$

This 2 × 30 rectangle contains 3 groups of 20 unit squares.

$$
30 = \quad 10 \quad + \quad 10 \quad + \quad 10
$$

2 · 2 × 10 = 20 ·	· 2 × 10 = 20 ·	· 2 × 10 = 20 · 2

$$
10 \quad + \quad 10 \quad + \quad 10
$$

This 2 × 30 rectangle contains 6 groups of 10 unit squares, so its area is 60 **square units**.

$$
30 = \quad 10 \quad + \quad 10 \quad + \quad 10
$$

1	1 × 10 = 10	1 × 10 = 10	1 × 10 = 10	1
1	1 × 10 = 10	1 × 10 = 10	1 × 10 = 10	1

$$
10 \quad + \quad 10 \quad + \quad 10
$$

3. How can we show this numerically? Complete the steps.

$2 \times 30 = (2 \times 1) \times (\underline{\quad} \times 10)$

$\quad = (\underline{\quad} \times \underline{\quad}) \times (1 \times 10)$

$\quad = \underline{\quad} \times 10 = 60$

4. On your MathBoard, draw a 30 × 2 rectangle and find its area.

5. How is the 30 × 2 rectangle similar to the 2 × 30 rectangle? How is it different?

Arrays and Area Models

▶ Use Place Value to Multiply

You have learned about the Base Ten Pattern in place value. This model shows how place value and multiplication are connected.

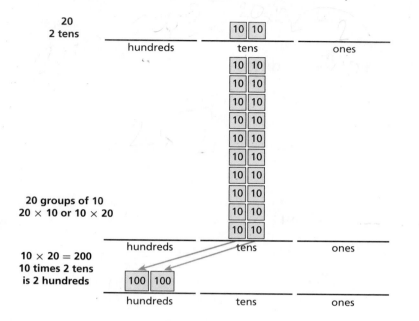

You can use properties to show the relationship between place value and multiplication.

Associative Property

$10 \times 20 = 10 \times (2 \times 10)$
$= (10 \times 2) \times 10$

Commutative Property

$= (2 \times 10) \times 10$

Associative Property

$= 2 \times (10 \times 10)$
$= 2 \times 100$
$= 200$

1. Ten times any number of tens gives you that number of hundreds. Complete the steps to show 10 times 5 tens.

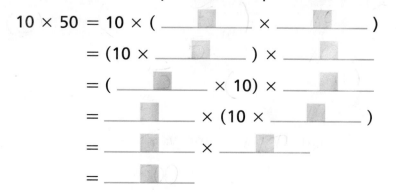

$10 \times 50 = 10 \times (\underline{\hspace{1.2cm}} \times \underline{\hspace{1.2cm}})$

$= (10 \times \underline{\hspace{1.2cm}}) \times \underline{\hspace{1.2cm}}$

$= (\underline{\hspace{1.2cm}} \times 10) \times \underline{\hspace{1.2cm}}$

$= \underline{\hspace{1.2cm}} \times (10 \times \underline{\hspace{1.2cm}})$

$= \underline{\hspace{1.2cm}} \times \underline{\hspace{1.2cm}}$

$= \underline{\hspace{1.2cm}}$

Use Activity
Workbook page 15.

▶ Model a Product of Tens

Olivia wants to tile the top of a table. The table is 20 inches by 30 inches. Olivia needs to find the area of the table in inches.

2. Find the area of this 20 × 30 rectangle by dividing it into 10-by-10 squares of 100.

3. Each tile is a 1-inch square. How many tiles does Olivia need to cover the tabletop?

4. Each box of tiles contains 100 tiles. How many boxes of tiles does Olivia need to buy?

▶ Factor the Tens

5. Complete the steps to show your work in Exercise 2 numerically.

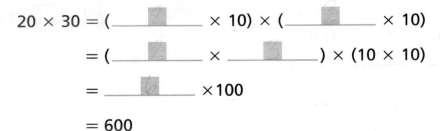

$$20 \times 30 = (\underline{\hspace{1cm}} \times 10) \times (\underline{\hspace{1cm}} \times 10)$$
$$= (\underline{\hspace{1cm}} \times \underline{\hspace{1cm}}) \times (10 \times 10)$$
$$= \underline{\hspace{1cm}} \times 100$$
$$= 600$$

6. Is it true that 20 × 30 = 30 × 20? Explain how you know.

Connect Place Value and Multiplication

Use Activity Workbook page 16.

VOCABULARY
factor
product

► **Look for Patterns**

Multiplying greater numbers in your head is easier when you learn patterns of multiplication with tens.

Start with column A and look for the patterns used to get the expressions in each column. Copy and complete the table.

Table 1

	A	B	C	D
	2 × 3	2 × 1 × 3 × 1	6 × 1	6
1.	2 × 30	2 × 1 × 3 × 10	6 × 10	
2.	20 × 30	2 × 10 × 3 × 10		

3. How are the expressions in column B different from the expressions in column A?

4. In column C, we see that each expression can be written as a number times a place value. Which of these **factors** gives more information about the size of the **product?**

5. Why is 6 the first digit of the products in column D?

6. Why are there different numbers of zeros in the products in column D?

Use Activity
Workbook page 17.

▶ Compare Tables

Copy and complete each table.

Table 2

	A	B	C	D
	6 × 3	6 × 1 × 3 × 1	18 × 1	18
7.	6 × 30	6 × 1 × 3 × 10	18 × 10	
8.	60 × 30	6 × 10 × 3 × 10		

Table 3

	A	B	C	D
	5 × 8	5 × 1 × 8 × 1	40 × 1	40
9.	5 × 80	5 × 1 × 8 × 10	40 × 10	
10.	50 × 80			

11. Why do the products in Table 2 have more digits than the products in Table 1?

12. Why are there more zeros in the products in Table 3 than the products in Table 2?

Mental Math and Multiplication

► **Explore the Area Model**

Use Activity Workbook page 18.

20	+	6
4 | (area model grid) |

1. How many square units of area are there in the tens part of the drawing?

2. What multiplication equation gives the area of the tens part of the drawing? Write this equation in its rectangle.

3. How many square units of area are there in the ones part?

4. What multiplication equation gives the area of the ones part? Write this equation in its rectangle.

5. What is the total of the two areas?

6. How do you know that 104 is the correct product of 4×26?

7. Read problems A and B.
   A. Al's photo album has 26 pages. Each page has 4 photos. How many photos are in Al's album?

   B. Nick took 4 photos. Henri took 26 photos. How many more photos did Henri take than Nick?

   Which problem could you solve using the multiplication you just did? Explain why.

▶ Use Rectangles to Multiply

Draw a rectangle for each problem on your MathBoard.
Find the tens product, the ones product, and the total.

Show your work on your paper or in your journal.

8. 3 × 28   9. 3 × 29   10. 5 × 30   11. 5 × 36

12. 4 × 38   13. 8 × 38   14. 4 × 28   15. 5 × 28

Solve each problem.

16. Maria's father planted 12 rows of tomatoes in his garden. Each row had 6 plants. How many tomato plants were in Maria's father's garden?

17. A library subscribes to 67 magazines. Each month the library receives 3 copies of each magazine. How many magazines does the library receive each month?

18. Complete this word problem. Then solve it.

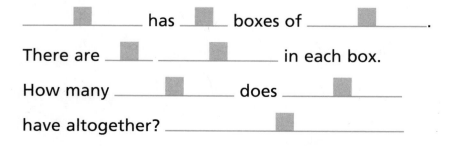

_____ has ____ boxes of _____.

There are ____ _____ in each box.

How many _____ does _____

have altogether? _____

Model One-Digit by Two-Digit Multiplication

▶ **Multiply One-Digit Dollar Amounts by Two-Digit Numbers**

Show your work on your paper or in your journal.

You can use your skills for multiplying a one-digit number by a two-digit number to multiply one-digit dollar amounts by two-digit numbers.

Find the exact cost. Give your answer in dollars.

19. A package of paper costs $2. If someone is purchasing 24 packages, how much will it cost?

20. A box lunch can be purchased for $3. How much will 83 lunches cost?

21. A movie ticket costs $8 per person. If 61 people go to the five o'clock show, how much money does the theater make for that show?

22. A round-trip train ticket costs $4 per person. If 58 fourth-graders take a class trip to the city on the train, how much will the train tickets cost altogether?

23. Admission to the zoo costs $5 per person. If a group of 72 students takes a trip to the zoo, how much will their tickets cost altogether?

24. Sara earns $9 per hour as a cashier. How much does she earn in a 40-hour week?

Show your work on your paper or in your journal.

▶ Multiply Two-Digit Dollar Amounts by One-Digit Numbers

You can use your skills for multiplying a one-digit number by a two-digit number to multiply one-digit numbers by two-digit dollar amounts.

Find the exact cost. Give your answer in dollars.

25. A bike costs $53. If 2 bikes are purchased, how much will be the total cost?

26. A store sells CDs for $14. If someone buys 7 of them, how much will they cost altogether?

27. An amusement park entrance fee is $23 per person. If 4 friends go to the amusement park, how much will their tickets cost altogether?

28. A hotel costs $72 per night. How much will it cost to stay 3 nights?

29. An airplane ticket costs $87. How much will 6 tickets cost?

30. Jorge earns $99 each week. He goes on vacation in 9 weeks. How much will he earn before his vacation?

Model One-Digit by Two-Digit Multiplication

VOCABULARY
estimate
rounding

▶ Estimate Products

It is easier to **estimate** the product of a two-digit number and a one-digit number when you think about the two multiples of ten close to the two-digit number. This is shown in the drawings below.

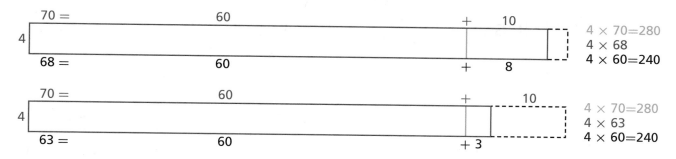

1. In each drawing, find the rectangles that represent 4×70 and 4×60. These rectangles "frame" the rectangles for 4×68 and 4×63. Find the values of 4×70 and 4×60.

   $4 \times 70 = $ ▨ $4 \times 60 = $ ▨

2. Look at the rectangle that represents 4×68. Is 4×68 closer to 4×60 or to 4×70? So is 4×68 closer to 240 or 280?

3. Look at the rectangle that represents 4×63. Is 4×63 closer to 4×60 or to 4×70? Is 4×63 closer to 240 or 280?

4. Explain how to use **rounding** to estimate the product of a one-digit number and a two-digit number.

2-5

Class Activity

Show your work on your paper or in your journal.

▶ Practice Estimation

Discuss how rounding and estimation could help solve these problems.

5. Keesha's school has 185 fourth-grade students. The library has 28 tables with 6 chairs at each table. Can all of the fourth-graders sit in the library at one time? How do you know?

6. Ameena is printing the class newsletter. There are 8 pages in the newsletter, and she needs 74 copies. Each package of paper contains 90 sheets. How many packages of paper does she need to print the newsletter?

Estimate each product. Then solve to check your estimate.

7. 3×52

8. 7×48

9. 9×27

10. 8×34

11. 8×35

12. 5×22

Estimate Products

VOCABULARY
Place Value Sections Method

▶ Use the Place Value Sections Method

You can use an area model to demonstrate the **Place Value Sections Method**. This strategy is used below for multiplying a one-digit number by a two-digit number.

Use Activity Workbook page 19.

Complete the steps.

27 =	20	+	7	
5	5 × 20 = 100		5 × 7 = 35	5

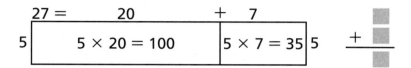

+

Use the Place Value Sections Method to solve the problem. Complete the steps.

1. The fourth-grade class is participating in a walk-a-thon. Each student will walk 8 laps around the track. There are 92 fourth-grade students. How many laps will the fourth-grade class walk?

Draw an area model and use the Place Value Sections Method to solve the problem.

2. A football coach is ordering 3 shirts for each football player. There are 54 players in the football program. How many shirts does the coach need to order for the entire program?

VOCABULARY
Expanded Notation Method

▶ Use the Expanded Notation Method

You can also use an area model to show how to use the **Expanded Notation Method**. Use the Expanded Notation Method to solve 5 × 27 below.

Use Activity Workbook page 20.

Complete the steps.

3.

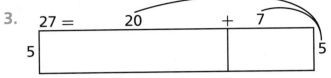

Use the Expanded Notation Method to solve the problem. Complete the steps.

4. A farm stand sold 4 bushels of apples in one day. Each bushel of apples weighs 42 pounds. How many pounds of apples did the farm stand sell?

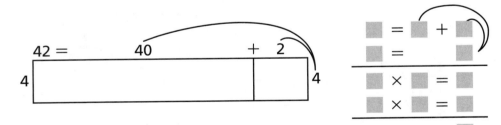

Draw an area model and use the Expanded Notation Method to solve the problem.

5. A marina needs to replace the boards on their pier. The pier is 7 feet by 39 feet. What is the area of the boards that need to be replaced?

VOCABULARY
Distributive Property
partial products

► Model the Distributive Property

You have used area models to help you multiply. You can use the area model to find 3 × 74 by writing 74 in expanded form and using the **Distributive Property** to find **partial products**. After you find all the partial products, you can add them together to find the actual product of 3 × 74.

Complete each exercise.

1. Write 74 in expanded form.

    3 × 74 = 3 (_____ + _____)

2. Use the Distributive Property.

    3 × 74 = (_____ × _____) + (_____ × _____)

The area models below show the steps to find the solution to 3 × 74.

STEP 1

74 = | 70 | + | 4 |
3 | 3 × 70 = 210 | | 3

Multiply the tens.

(3 × 70) = ▢

STEP 2

74 = | 70 | + | 4 |
3 | | 3 × 4 = 12 | 3

Multiply the ones.

(3 × 4) = ▢

STEP 3

74 = | 70 | + | 4 |
3 | 3 × 70 = 210 | 3 × 4 = 12 | 3

Add the partial products.

$$\begin{array}{r} 210 \\ + 12 \\ \hline \square \end{array}$$

3. What is the actual product of 3 × 74?

Use Activity
Workbook page 21.

VOCABULARY
Algebraic Notation Method

▶ Use the Algebraic Notation Method to Multiply

Another numerical multiplication method that can be represented by an area model is the **Algebraic Notation Method**. This method also decomposes the two-digit factor into tens and ones and then uses the Distributive Property.

Use the Algebraic Notation Method to solve each problem. Complete the steps.

4. 8 · 62

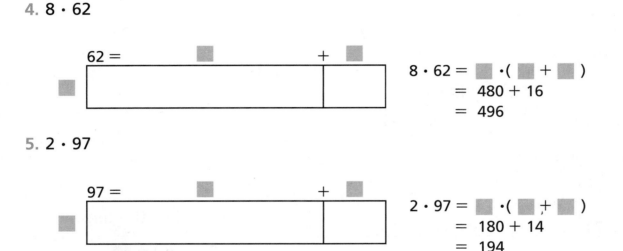

$8 \cdot 62 = \blacksquare \cdot (\blacksquare + \blacksquare)$
$= 480 + 16$
$= 496$

5. 2 · 97

$2 \cdot 97 = \blacksquare \cdot (\blacksquare + \blacksquare)$
$= 180 + 14$
$= 194$

Draw an area model and use the Algebraic Notation Method to solve the problem.

6. There are 9 members on the school's golf team. Each golfer hit a bucket of 68 golf balls at the driving range. How many golf balls did the entire team hit?

7. What is the first step in the Algebraic Notation Method?

Algebraic Notation Method

▶ Numerical Multiplication Methods

You have used the area model to help you multiply. In this lesson, you will compare the numerical multiplication methods that are related to this area model.

Place Value Sections Method

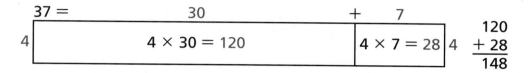

$37 =$ 30   +   7

4 | $4 \times 30 = 120$ | $4 \times 7 = 28$ | 4

$$\begin{array}{r} 120 \\ +\ 28 \\ \hline 148 \end{array}$$

Expanded Notation Method

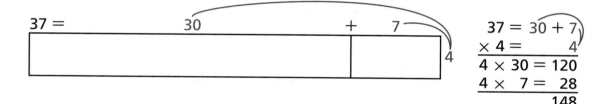

$37 =$ 30   +   7   4

$$\begin{array}{r} 37 = 30 + 7 \\ \times\ 4 = \qquad 4 \\ \hline 4 \times 30 = 120 \\ 4 \times\ 7 =\ \ 28 \\ \hline 148 \end{array}$$

Algebraic Notation Method

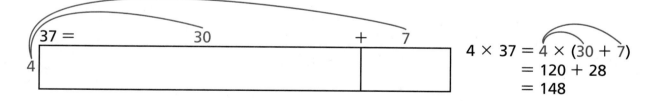

$37 =$ 30   +   7   4

$$\begin{aligned} 4 \times 37 &= 4 \times (30 + 7) \\ &= 120 + 28 \\ &= 148 \end{aligned}$$

▶ Connect the Multiplication Methods

Refer to the examples above.

1. What two values are added together to give the answer in all three methods?

2. What is different about the three methods?

Use Activity
Workbook page 22.

▶ Practice Different Methods

Fill in the blanks in the following solutions.

3. 4×86

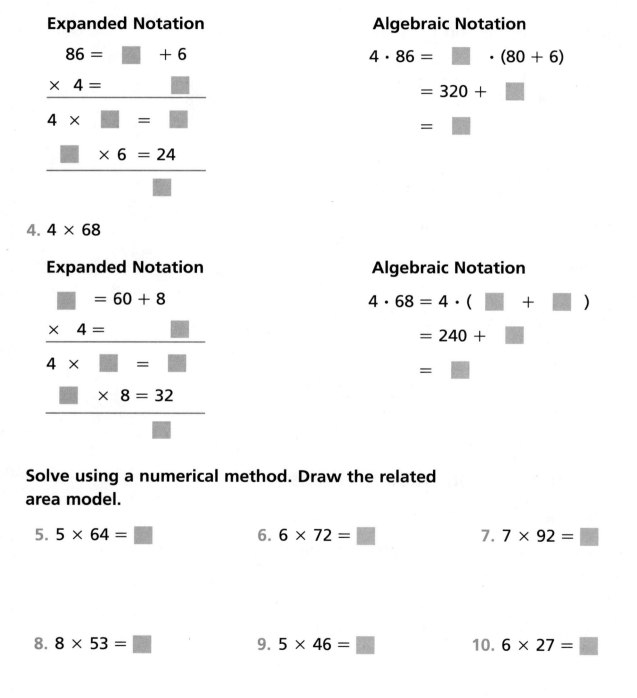

Expanded Notation

$$86 = \boxed{} + 6$$

$$\times\ \ 4 = \boxed{}$$
_____

$$4 \times \boxed{} = \boxed{}$$

$$\boxed{} \times 6 = 24$$
_____

$$\boxed{}$$

Algebraic Notation

$$4 \cdot 86 = \boxed{} \cdot (80 + 6)$$

$$= 320 + \boxed{}$$

$$= \boxed{}$$

4. 4×68

Expanded Notation

$$\boxed{} = 60 + 8$$

$$\times\ \ 4 = \boxed{}$$
_____

$$4 \times \boxed{} = \boxed{}$$

$$\boxed{} \times 8 = 32$$
_____

$$\boxed{}$$

Algebraic Notation

$$4 \cdot 68 = 4 \cdot (\ \boxed{}\ + \ \boxed{}\ )$$

$$= 240 + \boxed{}$$

$$= \boxed{}$$

Solve using a numerical method. Draw the related area model.

5. $5 \times 64 = \boxed{}$

6. $6 \times 72 = \boxed{}$

7. $7 \times 92 = \boxed{}$

8. $8 \times 53 = \boxed{}$

9. $5 \times 46 = \boxed{}$

10. $6 \times 27 = \boxed{}$

▶ Compare Multiplication Methods

Compare these methods for solving 9 × 28.

Method A	Method B	Method C	Method D
$28 = 20 + 8$	$28 = 20 + 8$	28	28
$\times\ 9 = \qquad 9$	$\times\ 9 = \qquad 9$	$\times\quad 9$	$\times\ 9$
$9 \times 20 = 180$	180	180	72
$9 \times 8 =\ \ 72$	72	72	180
252	252	252	252

1. How are all the methods similar? List at least two similarities.

2. How are the methods different? List at least three differences.

Discuss how the recording methods below show the partial products in different ways.

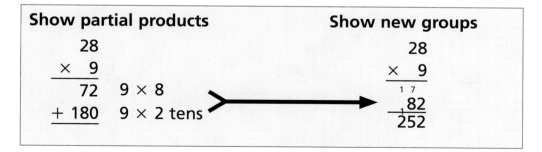

Show partial products

$$
\begin{array}{r}
28 \\
\times\ \ 9 \\
\hline
72 \quad 9 \times 8 \\
+\ 180 \quad 9 \times 2\ \text{tens}
\end{array}
$$

Show new groups

$$
\begin{array}{r}
28 \\
\times\ \ 9 \\
\hline
^{1\ 7} \\
82 \\
\hline
252
\end{array}
$$

2-9

Class Activity

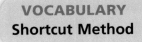

VOCABULARY
Shortcut Method

▶ Discuss the Shortcut Method

The steps for the Shortcut Method are shown below.

Shortcut Method with New Groups Above	
Method E:	

Step 1	Step 2
$\overset{7}{2}8$ $\times\ 9$ ___ 2	$\overset{7}{2}8$ $\times\ 9$ ___ 252

Shortcut Method with New Groups Below	
Method F:	

Step 1	Step 2
28 $\times\ 9$ ___ $^{7}2$	28 $\times\ 9$ ___ $^{7}252$

3. Where are the products 180 and 72 from Methods A–D?

▶ Practice Multiplication

Solve using any method. Sketch a rectangle if necessary.

4. 63
    × 5

5. 39
    × 8

6. 98
    × 2

7. 86
    × 4

8. 25
    × 7

9. 47
    × 9

10. 76
     × 3

11. 54
     × 6

60 UNIT 2 LESSON 9

Discuss Different Methods

► Use Rectangles to Multiply Hundreds

**You can use a model to show multiplication with hundreds.
Study this model to see how we can multiply 7 × 300.**

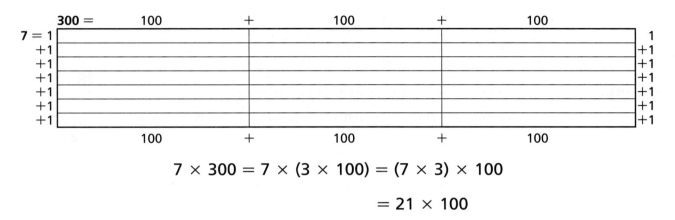

$$7 \times 300 = 7 \times (3 \times 100) = (7 \times 3) \times 100$$

$$= 21 \times 100$$

$$= 2{,}100$$

1. How many hundreds are represented in each column of
   the model?

2. How does knowing that $7 \times 3 = 21$ help you find
   7×300?

3. What property of multiplication is used in the equation,
   $7 \times (3 \times 100) = (7 \times 3) \times 100$?

4. Sketch a model of 6×400. Be ready to explain
   your model.

▶ Compare the Three Methods

You can use the **Place Value Sections Method** to multiply a one-digit number by a three-digit number.

237 =	200	+	30	+	7
4	4 × 200 = 800		4 × 30 = 120	4 × 7 = 28	4

$$\begin{array}{r} 800 \\ 120 \\ +\ \ 28 \\ \hline 948 \end{array}$$

5. What are the two steps used to find the product of 4 × 237 using the Place Value Sections Method.

The **Expanded Notation Method** uses the same steps as the Place Value Sections Method.

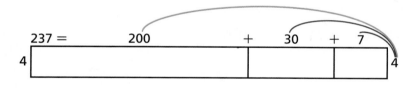

$$\begin{array}{r} 237 = 200 + 30 + 7 \\ \times\ 4 = \qquad\qquad\quad 4 \\ \hline 4 \times 200 = 800 \\ 4 \times 30 = 120 \\ 4 \times 7 = \ \ 28 \\ \hline 948 \end{array}$$

6. What is the last step in the Expanded Notation Method and the Place Value Sections Method?

The **Algebraic Notation Method** uses expanded form just like the other two methods. Even though the steps look different, they are the same as in the other methods.

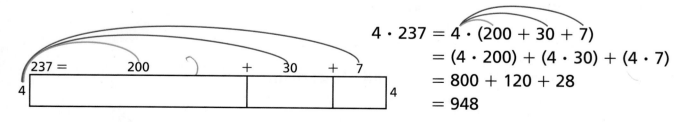

$$\begin{aligned} 4 \cdot 237 &= 4 \cdot (200 + 30 + 7) \\ &= (4 \cdot 200) + (4 \cdot 30) + (4 \cdot 7) \\ &= 800 + 120 + 28 \\ &= 948 \end{aligned}$$

7. What is the first step in all three methods?

▶ Practice Multiplication

Solve using any method. Show your work.
Draw an area model if necessary.

8. $7 \times 321 =$ ▨

9. $5 \times 218 =$ ▨

10. $612 \times 2 =$ ▨

11. $154 \times 6 =$ ▨

12. $236 \times 4 =$ ▨

13. $3 \times 273 =$ ▨

14. $482 \times 9 =$ ▨

15. $8 \times 615 =$ ▨

Show your work on your paper or in your journal.

▶ Multiplication With Dollar Amounts

You can use your skills for multiplying a one-digit number by a three-digit number to multiply one-digit dollar amounts by three-digit numbers and one-digit numbers by three-digit dollar amounts.

Find the exact cost. Give your answer in dollars.

16. A car tire costs $158. If Danica needs to buy new tires, how much will 4 tires cost?

17. The fourth grade is going on a field trip to the planetarium. A ticket costs $6. How much will it cost if 127 people go on the field trip?

18. A round-trip airplane ticket costs $224. If a group of 5 people buy tickets, how much will their tickets cost?

19. A book costs a bookstore $7 to order. If the store orders 325 copies of the book, how much does the store pay for the books?

20. During the summer, Joe makes $115 each week mowing lawns. How much will Joe make in 9 weeks?

21. A ticket to a show costs $8. There are 540 seats in the theater. If all the seats in the theater are occupied, how much money does the theater make for that show?

Show your work on your paper or in your journal.

▶ Discuss Problems With Too Much Information

A word problem may sometimes include more information than you need. Read the following problem and then answer each question.

Mrs. Sanchez is putting a border around her garden. Her garden is a rectangle with dimensions 12 feet by 18 feet. The border material costs $3.00 per foot. How many feet of border material is needed?

1. Identify any extra numerical information. Why isn't this information needed?

2. Solve the problem.

Solve each problem. Cross out information that is not needed.

3. Judy bought a CD for $10. It has 13 songs. Each song is 3 minutes long. How long will it take to listen to the whole CD?

4. Jerry has 64 coins in his coin collection and 22 stamps in his stamp collection. His sister has 59 stamps in her collection. How many stamps do they have altogether?

5. Adrian has been playing the piano for 3 years. He practices 20 minutes a day. He is preparing for a recital that is 9 days away. How many minutes of practice will he complete before the recital?

Show your work on your paper or in your journal.

▶ Discuss Problems With Too Little Information

When solving problems in real life, you need to determine what information is needed to solve the problem. Read the following problem and then answer each question.

The campers and staff of a day camp are going to an amusement park on a bus. Each bus holds 26 people. How many buses will be needed?

6. Do you have enough information to solve this problem? What additional information do you need?

Determine if the problem can be solved. If it cannot be solved, tell what information is missing. If it can be solved, solve it.

7. Richard is saving $5 a week to buy a bike. When will he have enough money?

8. Natalie wants to find out how much her cat weighs. She picks him up and steps on the scale. Together, they weigh 94 pounds. How much does the cat weigh?

9. Phyllis wants to make 8 potholders. She needs 36 loops for each potholder. How many loops does she need?

10. For one of the problems that could not be solved, rewrite it so it can be solved and then solve it.

Multistep Word Problems

Show your work on your paper or in your journal.

▶ Discuss Problems With Hidden Questions

Mrs. Norton bought 2 packages of white cheese with 8 slices in each pack. She bought 3 packages of yellow cheese with 16 slices in each pack. How many more slices of yellow cheese than white cheese did she buy?

11. What do you need to find?

12. What are the hidden questions?

13. Answer the hidden questions to solve the problem.

How many slices of white cheese? $2 \times 8 = $ ▨

How many slices of yellow cheese? $3 \times 16 = $ ▨

How many more slices of yellow cheese? $48 - 16 = $ ▨

Read the problem. Then answer the questions.

Maurice has 6 boxes of markers. June has 5 boxes of markers. Each box contains 8 markers. How many markers do Maurice and June have altogether?

14. Write the hidden questions.

15. Solve the problem.

> Show your work on your paper or in your journal.

► Mixed Problem Solving

Solve each problem and show your work.

16. Mr. Collins counts 54 cartons and 5 boxes of paper clips. Each carton contains 8 boxes. A box of paper clips costs $2. How many boxes of paper clips does he have?

17. Ms. Washington has 5 cartons of black printer ink. She has 4 cartons of color printer ink. Each carton contains 48 cartridges of ink. How many ink cartridges are there in all?

► What's the Error?

Dear Math Students,

My school is collecting cans for the annual food drive. There are 608 students in the entire school. A can of soup costs about $1. Each student will bring in 3 cans for the food drive. I wrote this multiplication to find the number of cans the school will collect in all.

I am not sure if my answer is correct. Can you help me?

Your friend,
Puzzled Penguin

$$\begin{array}{r} \overset{2}{6}08 \\ \times\quad 3 \\ \hline 1{,}864 \end{array}$$

18. Write a response to Puzzled Penguin.

► Compare Models

A coin-collecting book holds 24 coins on a page. There are 37 pages in the book. How many coins can the book hold? The models below all show the solution to 24 × 37.

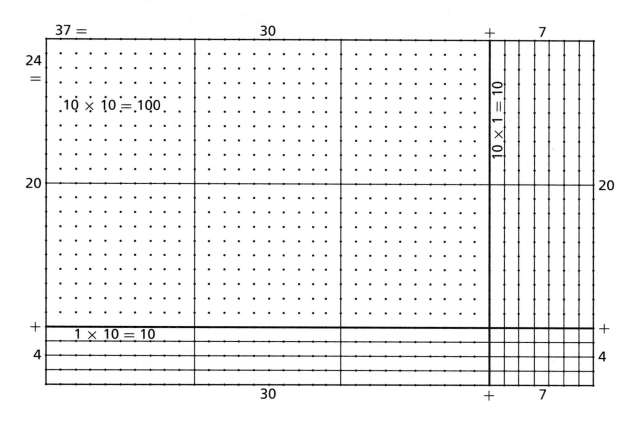

Area Model Sketch

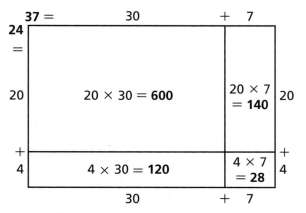

Place Value Sections Method

$$20 \times 30 = \mathbf{600}$$
$$20 \times 7 = \mathbf{140}$$
$$4 \times 30 = \mathbf{120}$$
$$\underline{4 \times 7 = \mathbf{28}}$$

1. Describe how each model shows 6 hundreds, 14 tens, 12 tens, and 28 ones.

▶ Investigate Products in the Sketch

Complete each equation.

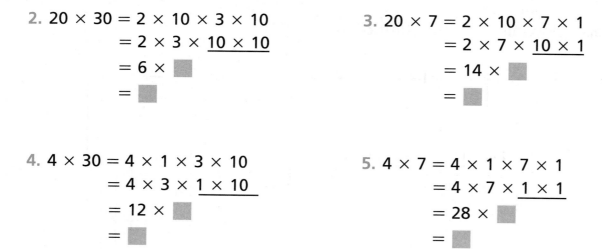

2. $20 \times 30 = 2 \times 10 \times 3 \times 10$
   $= 2 \times 3 \times \underline{10 \times 10}$
   $= 6 \times \blacksquare$
   $= \blacksquare$

3. $20 \times 7 = 2 \times 10 \times 7 \times 1$
   $= 2 \times 7 \times \underline{10 \times 1}$
   $= 14 \times \blacksquare$
   $= \blacksquare$

4. $4 \times 30 = 4 \times 1 \times 3 \times 10$
   $= 4 \times 3 \times \underline{1 \times 10}$
   $= 12 \times \blacksquare$
   $= \blacksquare$

5. $4 \times 7 = 4 \times 1 \times 7 \times 1$
   $= 4 \times 7 \times \underline{1 \times 1}$
   $= 28 \times \blacksquare$
   $= \blacksquare$

6. Explain how the underlined parts in Exercises 2–5 are shown in the dot drawing.

7. Find 24×37 by adding the products in Exercises 2–5.

▶ Practice and Discuss Modeling

Use your MathBoard to sketch an area drawing for each exercise. Then find the product.

8. 36×58

9. 28×42

10. 63×27

11. 26×57

12. 86×35

13. 38×65

▶ Compare Multiplication Methods

Each area model is the same. Study how these three methods of recording 43 × 67 are related to the area models.

Place Value Sections Method

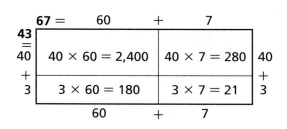

$$40 \times 60 = 2,400$$
$$40 \times 7 = 280$$
$$3 \times 60 = 180$$
$$\underline{3 \times 7 = + 21}$$
$$2,881$$

Expanded Notation Method

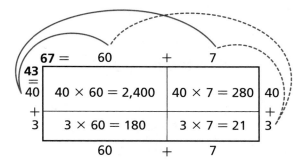

$$\begin{array}{r} 67 \quad (60 + 7 \\ \times\ 43 = 40 + 3 \\ \hline \end{array}$$
$$40 \times 60 = 2,400$$
$$40 \times 7 = 280$$
$$3 \times 60 = 180$$
$$\underline{3 \times 7 = 21}$$
$$2,881$$

Algebraic Notation Method

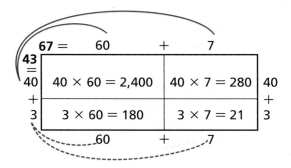

$$43 \cdot 67 = (40 + 3) \cdot (60 + 7)$$
$$= 2,400 + 280 + 180 + 21$$
$$= 2,881$$

1. What is alike about all the three methods?

▶ Other Ways to Record Multiplication

Discuss how the recording methods below show the partial products in different ways.

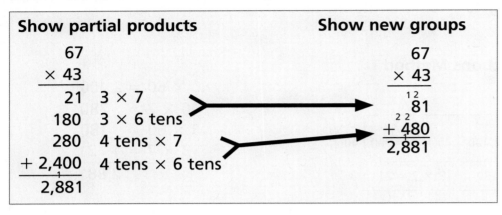

Show partial products	Show new groups
67	67
× 43	× 43
21 3 × 7	81
180 3 × 6 tens	+ 480
280 4 tens × 7	2,881
+ 2,400 4 tens × 6 tens	
2,881	

▶ The Shortcut Method

The steps for the Shortcut Method are shown below.

New Groups Above

Step 1	Step 2	Step 3	Step 4	Step 5
2	2	2 2	2 2	2 2
67	67	67	67	67
× 43	× 43	× 43	× 43	× 43
1	201	201	201	201
		8	268	+ 268
				2,881

New Groups Below

Step 1	Step 2	Step 3	Step 4	Step 5
67	67	67	67	67
× 43	× 43	× 43	× 43	× 43
1	201	201	201	201
		8	268	+ 268
				2,881

Discuss how the area drawing below relates to the Shortcut Method.

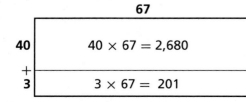

	67
40	40 × 67 = 2,680
+ 3	3 × 67 = 201

▶ Estimate Products

Two-digit products can be estimated by rounding each number to the nearest ten.

Estimate and then solve.

1. 28 × 74   2. 84 × 27   3. 93 × 57

4. 87 × 54   5. 38 × 62   6. 65 × 39

7. 26 × 43   8. 59 × 96   9. 53 × 74

10. Write a multiplication word problem. Estimate the product and then solve.

11. Would using an estimate be problematic in the situation you wrote for Exercise 10? Explain why or why not.

► What's the Error?

Dear Math Students,

My friends and I are helping build flower boxes for a community garden. We are going to build 42 flower boxes. The building plans say each box needs 13 nails. I rounded to estimate how many nails we'll need. Since 40 x 10 = 400, I bought a box of 400 nails.

My friends say we won't have enough nails. Did I make a mistake? Can you help me estimate how many nails we need?

Your friend,
Puzzled Penguin

12. Write a response to Puzzle Penguin.

Show your work on your paper or in your journal.

Estimate and then solve. Explain whether the estimate is problematic in each situation.

13. Sally's family is taking an 18-day vacation and needs to have someone take care of their cat. A veterinarian charges $14 per day to care for the cat. How much money do they need to save to care for the cat?

14. An artist uses 47 tiles to make a mosaic. The artist needs to make 21 mosaics for a fair. How many tiles does the artist need to buy?

Check Products of Two-Digit Numbers

► Practice Multiplication Methods

1. Multiply 38 × 59.

Shortened Expanded Notation Method	**Shortcut Method**
38 × 59	38 × 59

Solve using any method and show your work.
Check your work with estimation.

2. 43 × 22

3. 25 × 15

4. 31 × 62

5. 54 × 72

6. 81 × 33

7. 49 × 62

► **Practice Multiplication**

With practice, you will be able to solve a multiplication problem using fewer written steps.

Show your work on your paper or in your journal.

Solve.

8. Between his ninth and tenth birthdays, Jimmy read 1 book each week. There are 52 weeks in a year. If each book had about 95 pages, about how many pages did he read during the year?

9. Sam's father built a stone wall in their back yard. The wall was 14 stones high and 79 stones long. How many stones did he use to build the wall?

10. Balloon Bonanza sells party balloons in packages of 25 balloons. There are 48 packages in the store. How many balloons are in 48 packages?

11. Brian is buying T-shirts for the marching band. He knows that at parades the band forms 24 rows. Each row has 13 students. If T-shirts come in boxes of 100, how many boxes of T-shirts should Brian buy?

▶ Use Rectangles to Multiply Thousands

You can use a model to multiply greater numbers.
Notice that each of the smaller rectangles in this model
represents one thousand. Each of the columns represents
seven one-thousands or 7,000.

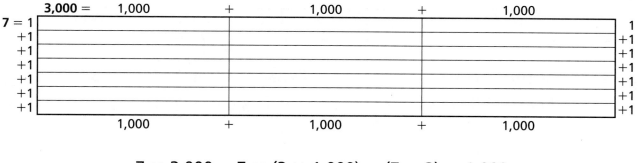

$$7 \times 3{,}000 = 7 \times (3 \times 1{,}000) = (7 \times 3) \times 1{,}000$$
$$= 21 \times 1{,}000$$
$$= 21{,}000$$

1. While multiplying by thousands, how many zeros can
   you expect in the product?

2. How does thinking of 3,000 as $3 \times 1{,}000$ help you to
   multiply $7 \times 3{,}000$?

3. Draw a model for $4 \times 8{,}000$. Then find the product.

► Compare Multiplication Methods

You can use the multiplication methods you have learned to multiply a one-digit number by a four-digit number.

Find 8 × 3,248.

3,248 =	3,000	+	200	+	40	+	8	
8								8

Place Value Sections Method

$$8 \times 3,000 = 24,000$$
$$8 \times 200 = 1,600$$
$$8 \times 40 = 320$$
$$\underline{8 \times 8 = 64}$$
$$25,984$$

Expanded Notation Method

$$3,248 = 3,000 + 200 + 40 + 8$$
$$\times 8 = 8$$
$$\overline{8 \times 3,000 = 24,000}$$
$$8 \times 200 = 1,600$$
$$8 \times 40 = 320$$
$$\underline{8 \times 8 = 64}$$
$$25,984$$

Algebraic Notation Method

$$8 \times 3,248 = 8 \times (3,000 + 200 + 40 + 8)$$
$$= (8 \times 3,000) + (8 \times 200) + (8 \times 40) + (8 \times 8)$$
$$= 24,000 + 1,600 + 320 + 64$$
$$= 25,984$$

Make a rectangle drawing for each problem on your MathBoard. Then solve the problem using the method of your choice.

4. $3 \times 8,153 =$ ▨

5. $4 \times 2,961 =$ ▨

6. $6 \times 5,287 =$ ▨

7. $7 \times 1,733 =$ ▨

► Compare Methods of Multiplication

Look at the drawing and the five numerical solutions for 4 × 2,237.

2,237 =   2,000   +   200   +   30   +   7

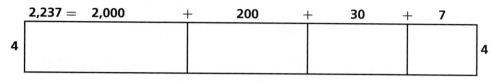

4 | | | | | 4

Method A	Method B	Method C	Method D	Method E	Method F
2,237 = 2,000 + 200 + 30 + 7	2,237 = 2,000 + 200 + 30 + 7	2,237	2,237	1 2 2,237	2,237
× 4 = 4	× 4 = 4	× 4	× 4	× 4	× 4
4 × 2,000 = 8,000	8,000	8,000	28	8,948	+2
4 × 200 = 800	800	800	120		8,948
4 × 30 = 120	120	120	800		
4 × 7 = 28	28	28	8,000		
8,948	8,948	8,948	8,948		

1. How are the solutions similar? List at least two ways.

2. How are the solutions different? List at least three comparisons between methods.

3. How do Methods A–D relate to the drawing? List at least two ways.

▶ Analyze the Shortcut Method

Look at this breakdown of solution steps for Method E and Method F.

Method E			
Step 1	**Step 2**	**Step 3**	**Step 4**
$\overset{2}{2{,}2\overset{}{3}7}$	$\overset{1\,2}{2{,}2\overset{}{3}7}$	$\overset{1\,2}{2{,}2\overset{}{3}7}$	$\overset{1\,2}{2{,}2\overset{}{3}7}$
$\times \quad 4$	$\times \quad 4$	$\times \quad 4$	$\times \quad 4$
8	48	948	8,948

Method F			
Step 1	**Step 2**	**Step 3**	**Step 4**
$2{,}237$	$2{,}237$	$2{,}237$	$2{,}237$
$\times \underset{2}{\quad 4}$	$\times \underset{1\,2}{\quad 4}$	$\times \underset{1\,2}{\quad 4}$	$\times \underset{1\,2}{\quad 4}$
8	48	948	8,948

4. Describe what happens in Step 1.

5. Describe what happens in Step 2.

6. Describe what happens in Step 3.

7. Describe what happens in Step 4.

Use the Shortcut Method

► Round and Estimate With Thousands and Hundreds

You can use what you know about rounding and multiplication with thousands to estimate the product of 4 × 3,692.

8. Find the product if you round up: 4 × 4,000 = ▢

9. Find the product if you round down: 4 × 3,000 = ▢

10. Which one of the two estimates will be closer to the actual solution? Why?

Show your work on your paper or in your journal.

11. Calculate the actual solution.

12. Explain why neither estimate is very close to the actual solution.

13. What would be the estimate if you added 4 × 600 to 4 × 3,000; (4 × 3,000) + (4 × 600)?

14. What would be the estimate if you added 4 × 700 to 4 × 3,000; (4 × 3,000) + (4 × 700)?

15. Estimate 4 × 7,821 by rounding 7,821 to the nearest thousand.

16. Find the actual product.

17. Find a better estimate for 4 × 7,821. Show your work.

Round, estimate, and fix the estimate as needed.

18. 6 × 3,095

19. 7 × 2,784

▶ Estimate Products

You can use estimation to decide if an answer is reasonable.

Solve and then estimate to check if your answer is reasonable. Show your estimate.

20. 5 × 3,487 = ▧

21. 7 × 8,894 = ▧

22. 4 × 7,812 = ▧

23. 3 × 4,109 = ▧

▶ What's the Error?

Dear Math Students,

My school collected 2,468 empty cartons of milk during the day today. If the school collects about the same number of cartons each day for 5 days, I estimated that the school will collect 17,500 empty cartons of milk. I wrote this estimate.

$$(5 \times 3,000) + (5 \times 500) = 17,500$$

I am not sure if this is a reasonable estimate. Can you help me?

Your Friend,
Puzzled Penguin

24. Write a response to Puzzled Penguin.

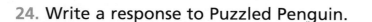

Use the Shortcut Method

► Practice Mixed Multiplication

Solve using any method and show your work. Check your work with estimation.

1. 35 × 9

2. 56 × 17

3. 228 × 2

4. 23
   × 7

5. 77
   × 9

6. 59
   × 3

7. 92
   × 84

8. 49
   × 12

9. 61
   × 36

10. 459
    ×   4

11. 588
    ×   6

12. 216
    ×   7

13. 3,473
    ×   5

14. 1,156
    ×   8

15. 2,937
    ×   3

▶ Practice with Word Problems

Solve using any method and show your work.
Check your work with estimation.

Show your work
on your paper or
in your journal.

16. The lines on a doubles tennis court are painted to be
78 feet long and 36 feet wide. The lines on a singles
tennis court are painted to be 78 feet long and 27 feet
wide. What is the difference between the areas of a
doubles tennis court and a singles tennis court?

17. A movie theater has 287 crates of popcorn. Each crate
holds 8 pounds of popcorn. There are 13 people who
work at the theater. How many pounds of popcorn
are there altogether?

18. Jenny goes to a 55-minute-long dance class 3 days each
week. There are 9 weeks until the class recital. How
many minutes of dance class are there until the recital?

19. Alex is shopping for school clothes. He buys 4 shirts
for $12 each. He also buys 3 pairs of shorts for $17
each. How much does Alex spend on school clothes
in all?

20. Casey draws a rectangular array that is 1,167 units
long and 7 units wide. What is the area of
Casey's array?

Show your work on your paper or in your journal.

► **Math and Games**

This is a game called *Big City Building*. The goal of the game is to design and build a successful city within a budget. To win the game, the city must have all of the features of a real-life city such as apartments, schools, parks, and shops, so its residents will be happy.

1. Each city in *Big City Building* requires a fire station, a police station, and a post office. These each cost $2,657 in taxes per year to maintain. How much does it cost to maintain the fire station, the police station, and the post office building for one year?

2. In *Big City Building*, the roads are standard two-lane roads. The total width of the road is 9 meters. If each block is 82 meters long, what is the area of the road of one city block in square meters?

▶ Big City Building

The table shows the cost of different features on the *Big City Building* game. Below is Scott's design, so far, for his city in *Big City Building*.

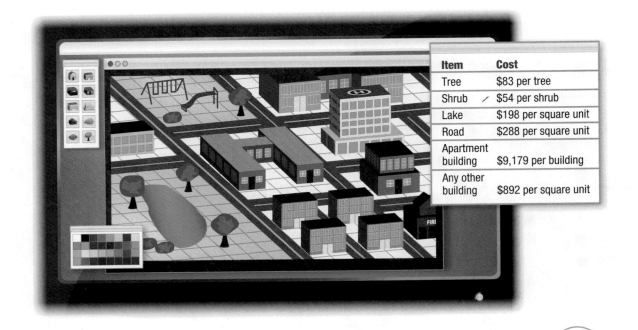

Item	Cost
Tree	$83 per tree
Shrub ✓	$54 per shrub
Lake	$198 per square unit
Road	$288 per square unit
Apartment building	$9,179 per building
Any other building	$892 per square unit

Currently, Scott has $156,324 in *Big City Building* money to create his city.

Show your work on your paper or in your journal.

3. Scott buys 42 trees to put in the park. The trees cost $83 each. How much money does Scott pay for the trees?

4. Each apartment building contains 59 apartment units. Scott has 4 apartment buildings in his city. How many apartment units does Scott's city have?

5. If Scott's city is 27 units long and 19 units wide, what is the area of Scott's city in square units?

Focus on Mathematical Practices

Use the Activity Workbook Unit Test on pages 23–26.

VOCABULARY
Distributive Property
estimate
partial products
rounding

▶ Vocabulary

Choose the best term from the box.

1. _____ are the products of the ones, tens, hundreds, and so on in multidigit multiplication. (Lessons 2-7)

2. An _____ is a number close to an exact amount. (Lesson 2-5)

3. The _____ lets you find a number times a sum by multiplying the number by each addend and then adding the products. (Lessons 2-7)

▶ Concepts and Skills

4. Write the steps for finding 50 × 30 by factoring the tens. (Lesson 2-2)

5. Explain how you know that 10 × 60 = 600. (Lesson 2-2)

6. Explain how the Expanded Notation Method is similar to the Place Value Sections Method when multiplying a one-digit number by a two-digit number. (Lesson 2-6)

7. Use mental math to find each product. (Lesson 2-3)

   4 × 7   4 × 700

   4 × 70   4 × 7,000

   40 × 70

Multiply using any method. Show your work.
(Lessons 2-8, 2-10, 2-14)

8. 3×68

9. 5×84

10. 3×506

11. 9×265

12. 16×50

13. 12×32

14. $6 \times 4,518$

15. $4 \times 2,706$

Estimate each product. Solve to check your estimate.
(Lessons 2-5, 2-14, 2-17)

16. 7 × 82

17. 33 × 66

18. 46 × 20

19. 9 × 3,276

▶ Problem Solving

Find the exact cost. (Lessons 2-4, 2-10)

20. A rental car costs $63 per day. If someone rents the car for 6 days, how much will be the total cost?

21. The Adventure Club is going skating. The price of admission to the skating rink is $3 per person. If there are 214 people in the club, how much will it cost the club to skate?

22. A travel agent is booking flights for a group of 9 people. If each airplane ticket costs $184, how much will their tickets cost altogether?

Solve each problem. List any extra numerical information.
(Lesson 2-15)

23. Mariah is painting wall murals in the cafeteria. One mural is 12 feet by 28 feet. The other mural is 12 feet by 32 feet. What is the total area of the cafeteria that Mariah is painting?

24. A family spent 7 hours at the zoo. They bought 2 adult tickets for $20 each and 3 child tickets for $10 each. They bought lunch for $23. How much did the tickets cost?

25. **Extended Response** Sketch an area model for the product 6 × 3,243. Explain how the area model can be used to find the product. (Lesson 2-16)

Family Letter

Dear Family,

Your child is familiar with multiplication from earlier units. Unit 3 of *Math Expressions* extends the concepts used in multiplication to teach your child division. The main goals of this unit are to:

• Learn methods for dividing whole numbers up to four digits.

• Use estimates to check the reasonableness of answers.

• Solve problems involving division and remainders.

Your child will learn and practice techniques such as the Place Value Sections, Expanded Notation, and Digit-by-Digit methods to gain speed and accuracy in division. At first, your child will learn to use patterns and multiplication to divide. Later, your child will learn to use the methods with divisors from 2 to 9. Then your child will learn to divide when there is a zero in the quotient or dividend and to watch out for potential problems involving these situations.

Share with your family the Family Letter on Activity Workbook page 27.

Your child may use whatever method he or she chooses as long as he or she can explain it. Some children like to use different methods.

Examples of Division Methods:

Place Value Sections Method	Expanded Notation Method	Digit-by-Digit Method
$60 + 6 = 66$	$\begin{array}{r} 6 \\ 60 \end{array}\Big]\,66$	66
$5\,\big|\, \begin{array}{c c} 330 & 30 \\ -300 & 30 \\ \hline 30 & 0 \end{array}$	$5\overline{)330}$ -300 $\overline{30}$ -30 $\overline{0}$	$5\overline{)330}$ $-\,30$ $\overline{30}$ $-\,30$ $\overline{0}$

Your child will also learn to interpret remainders in the context of the problem being solved; for example, when the remainder alone is the answer to a word problem.

Finally, your child will apply this knowledge to solve mixed problems with one or more steps and using all four operations.

If you have questions or problems, please contact me.

Sincerely,
Your child's teacher

COMMON CORE

This unit includes the Common Core Standards for Mathematical Content for Numbers and Operations in Base Ten, 4.NBT.6 and all Mathematical Practices.

Estimada familia:

En unidades anteriores su niño se ha familiarizado con la multiplicación. La Unidad 3 de *Math Expressions* amplía los conceptos usados en la multiplicación para que su niño aprenda la división. Los objetivos principales de esta unidad son:

• aprender métodos para dividir números enteros de hasta cuatro dígitos.

• usar la estimación para comprobar si las respuestas son razonables.

• resolver problemas que requieran división y residuos.

Su niño aprenderá y practicará técnicas tales como las de Secciones de valor posicional, Notación extendida y Dígito por dígito, para adquirir rapidez y precisión en la división. Al principio, su niño aprenderá a usar patrones y la multiplicación para dividir. Más adelante, usará los métodos con divisores de 2 a 9. Luego, aprenderá a dividir cuando haya un cero en el cociente o en el dividendo, y a detectar problemas que pueden surgir en esas situaciones.

Ejemplos de métodos de división:

Secciones de valor posicional	Notación extendida	Dígito por dígito

Secciones de valor posicional

$$60 + 6 = 66$$

5	330	30
	− 300	30
	30	0

Notación extendida

$$\begin{array}{r} 6 \\ 60 \rceil 66 \\ 5\overline{)330} \\ -300 \\ \overline{30} \\ -30 \\ \overline{0} \end{array}$$

Dígito por dígito

$$\begin{array}{r} 66 \\ 5\overline{)330} \\ -30 \\ \overline{30} \\ -30 \\ \overline{0} \end{array}$$

Muestra a tu familia la Carta a la familia de la página 28 del Cuaderno de actividades y trabajo.

Su niño también aprenderá a interpretar los residuos en el contexto del problema que se esté resolviendo; por ejemplo, cuando solamente el residuo es la respuesta a un problema.

Su niño puede usar el método que elija siempre y cuando pueda explicarlo. A algunos niños les gusta usar métodos diferentes.

Por último, su niño aplicará este conocimiento para resolver problemas mixtos de uno o más pasos, usando las cuatro operaciones.

Si tiene alguna pregunta o comentario, por favor comuníquese conmigo.

Atentamente,
El maestro de su niño

COMMON CORE Esta unidad incluye los Common Core Standards for Mathematical Content for Numbers and Operations in Base Ten, 4.NBT.6 and all Mathematical Practices.

Divide With Remainders

▶ Division Vocabulary and Models

Although multiplication and division are inverse operations, each operation has its own language.

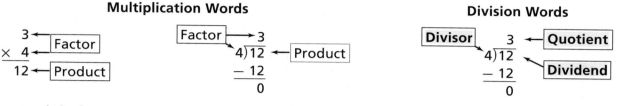

The models for multiplication and division are the same models.

array	rows and columns	area model

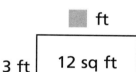

12 bottles on a table

$12 \div 3 = \blacksquare$

$3 \times \blacksquare = 12$

12 tiles on a wall

$12 \div 3 = \blacksquare$

$3 \times \blacksquare = 12$

12 square feet of carpet

$12 \div 3 = \blacksquare$

$3 \times \blacksquare = 12$

▶ Discuss Remainders

Sometimes when you divide, some are left over. The left over amount is called the **remainder**.

If you have 14 juice boxes arranged in groups of 3, how many juice boxes will be left over?

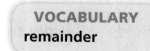

$$\begin{array}{r} 4R2 \\ 3\overline{)14} \\ -12 \\ \hline 2 \end{array}$$

2 are left over.
2 is the remainder.

Compare the divisor and the remainder. The remainder must be less than the divisor.

$2 < 3$, so the remainder is correct.

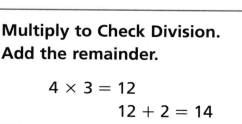

Multiply to Check Division.
Add the remainder.

$$4 \times 3 = 12$$
$$12 + 2 = 14$$

Use Activity Workbook page 29.

▶ **Divide with Remainders**

The remainder must be less than the divisor.
If it is not, increase the quotient.

```
    3                    4 R3
5)23        ⟶      5)23
 -15                  -20
    8 no                 3 yes
    8 > 5              3 < 5
```

```
    8                    9 R6
9)87        ⟶      9)87
 -72                  -81
   15 no                6 yes
   15 > 9             6 < 9
```

Divide with remainders.

1. 2)19   2. 7)50   3. 9)48

4. 5)48   5. 6)19   6. 3)25

Divide. Multiply to check the last problem in each row.

7. 6)27   8. 4)30   9. $\begin{array}{r} 5\ R4 \\ 7\overline{)39} \\ -35 \\ \hline 4 \end{array}$ 7 · 5 + 4 =
                                                                                                                            35 + 4 = 39

10. 8)43   11. 5)26   12. 9)41

13. 5)32   14. 4)21   15. 3)22

▶ Multiply and Divide with Zeros

When you multiply or divide with zeros, you can see a pattern.

$4 \times 1 = 4$	$4 \div 4 = 1$	$7 \times 5 = 35$	$35 \div 7 = 5$
$4 \times 10 = 40$	$40 \div 4 = 10$	$7 \times 50 = 350$	$350 \div 7 = 50$
$4 \times 100 = 400$	$400 \div 4 = 100$	$7 \times 500 = 3,500$	$3,500 \div 7 = 500$
$4 \times 1,000 = 4,000$	$4,000 \div 4 = 1,000$	$7 \times 5,000 = 35,000$	$35,000 \div 7 = 5,000$

16. What pattern do you notice when you multiply with zeros?

17. What pattern do you notice when you divide with zeros?

Find the unknown factor. Multiply to check the division.

18. $4\overline{)320}$ $4 \cdot \boxed{80} = 320$

19. $6\overline{)420}$ $6 \cdot \boxed{70} = 420$

20. $7\overline{)49}$ $7 \cdot \boxed{} = 49$

21. $3\overline{)1,800}$ $3 \cdot \boxed{} = 1,800$

22. $5\overline{)4,500}$ $5 \cdot \boxed{} = 4,500$

23. $9\overline{)3,600}$ $9 \cdot \boxed{} = 3,600$

24. $6\overline{)3,000}$ $6 \cdot \boxed{} = 3,000$

25. $5\overline{)4,000}$ $5 \cdot \boxed{} = 4,000$

► Divide With Zeros and Remainders

Divide. Multiply to check your answer.

26.
$$
\begin{array}{r}
300 \text{ R6} \\
7\overline{)2{,}106} \\
-2{,}100 \\
\hline
6
\end{array}
$$

27. $8\overline{)643}$

28. $9\overline{)275}$

29. $2\overline{)1{,}601}$

30. $3\overline{)1{,}802}$

31. $4\overline{)2{,}803}$

32. $5\overline{)4{,}503}$

33. $6\overline{)4{,}205}$

> Use Activity
> Workbook page 30.

► Multiplying and Dividing

Complete the steps.

1. Sam divides 738 by 6. He uses the Place Value
   Sections Method and the Expanded Notation Method.

   a. Sam thinks: I'll draw the Place Value Sections that I know from
      multiplication. To divide, I need to find how many hundreds,
      tens, and ones to find the unknown factor.

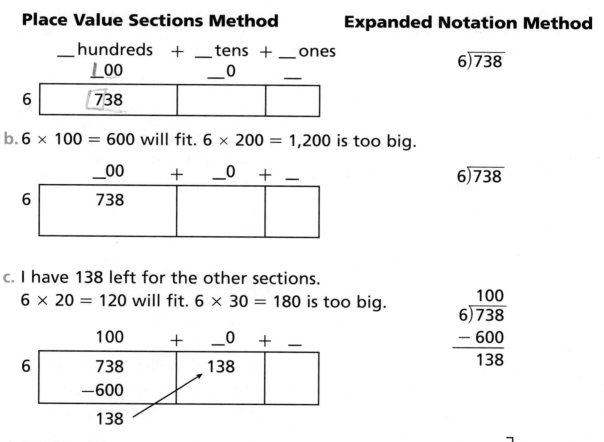

   b. $6 \times 100 = 600$ will fit. $6 \times 200 = 1{,}200$ is too big.

   c. I have 138 left for the other sections.
      $6 \times 20 = 120$ will fit. $6 \times 30 = 180$ is too big.

   d. $6 \times 3 = 18$

Use Activity
Workbook page 31.

▶ Practice the Place Value Sections Method

Solve. Use Place Value Sections Method for division.

The sidewalk crew knows that the new sidewalk at the mall will be 3,915 square feet. It will be 9 feet wide. How long will it be?

$$\underline{400} + \underline{30} + \underline{5} = 435$$

	3,915	315	45
9 ft	−3,600	−270	−45
	315	45	0

2. The sidewalk at the theater will be 2,748 square feet. It will be 6 feet wide. How long will it be?

$$\_00 + \_0 + \_ = \_\_\_$$

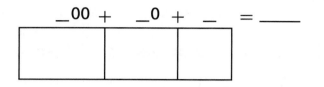

3. Pens are packaged in boxes of 8. The store is charged for a total of 4,576 pens. How many boxes of pens did they receive?

$$\_00 + \_0 + \_ = \_\_\_$$

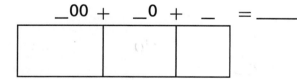

4. A factory has 2,160 erasers. They package them in groups of 5. How many packages of erasers does the factory have?

$$\_\_ + \_\_ + \_ = \_\_\_$$

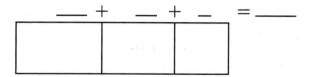

5. A party planner has 834 small flowers to make party favors. She will put 3 flowers in each party favor. How many party favors can she make?

$$\_\_\_ + \_\_ + \_ = \_\_\_$$

6. An artist has 956 tiles to use in a design. He plans to arrange the tiles in group of 4 tiles. How many groups of 4 tiles can he make?

$$\_\_\_ + \_\_ + \_ = \_\_\_$$

Show your work
on your paper or
in your journal.

► Problem Solving with 3-Digit Quotients

Solve using the Expanded Notation Method for division.

7. A toy company has 740 games to donate to different schools. Each school will receive 4 games. How many schools will receive games?

8. A landscape architect designs a rectangular garden that is 1,232 square feet. It is 8 feet wide. How long is the garden?

9. The convention center is expecting 1,434 people for an event. Since each table can seat 6 people, how many tables will the convention center need to set up?

10. An adult lion weighs an average of 375 pounds. A lion cub weighs an average of 3 pounds at birth. How many times more does the adult lion weigh than the lion cub weighs at birth?

▶ Practice with the Expanded Notation Method

Solve using the Expanded Notation Method for division.

11. 3)552

12. 7)851

13. 2)978

14. 4)979

15. 3)1,098

16. 5)2,945

17. 7)1,652

18. 8)4,520

19. 6)3,938

Use Activity
Workbook page 32.

▶ 2-Digit and 4-Digit Quotients

Solve. Use the Place Value Sections and the Expanded Notation Methods for division.

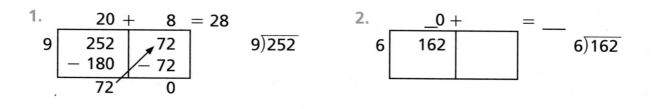

1.

```
        20  +     8   = 28
   9 | 252  |  72
     | -180 | - 72
        72      0
```

9)252

2.

```
        _0 +        = _
   6 | 162  |
```

6)162

3.

```
      _,000 +    _00 +    _0 +    _   =
   8 | 8,984 |        |        |
```

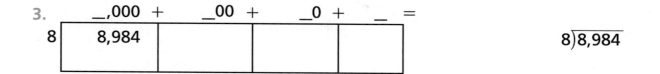

8)8,984

4.

```
      _,000 +    _00 +    _0 +    _ =
   3 | 7,722 |        |        |
```

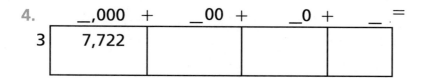

3)7,722

► **Finding Group Size**

5. An orchard has 516 apples ready for delivery. There are the same number of apples in each of 4 crates. How many apples are in each crate?

516 ÷ 4 = ?

4)516

Divide 5 hundreds, 1 ten, 6 ones equally among 4 groups.

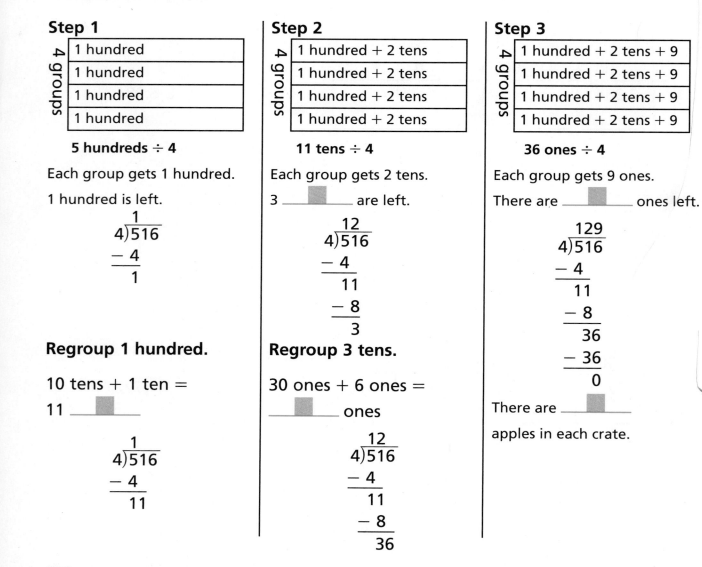

Complete the steps.

Step 1

4 groups	1 hundred
	1 hundred
	1 hundred
	1 hundred

5 hundreds ÷ 4

Each group gets 1 hundred.

1 hundred is left.

```
     1
4)516
  - 4
    1
```

Regroup 1 hundred.

10 tens + 1 ten =

11 _____

```
     1
4)516
  - 4
   11
```

Step 2

4 groups	1 hundred + 2 tens
	1 hundred + 2 tens
	1 hundred + 2 tens
	1 hundred + 2 tens

11 tens ÷ 4

Each group gets 2 tens.

3 _____ are left.

```
    12
4)516
  - 4
   11
  - 8
    3
```

Regroup 3 tens.

30 ones + 6 ones =

_____ ones

```
    12
4)516
  - 4
   11
  - 8
   36
```

Step 3

4 groups	1 hundred + 2 tens + 9
	1 hundred + 2 tens + 9
	1 hundred + 2 tens + 9
	1 hundred + 2 tens + 9

36 ones ÷ 4

Each group gets 9 ones.

There are _____ ones left.

```
   129
4)516
  - 4
   11
  - 8
   36
  - 36
    0
```

There are _____

apples in each crate.

Discuss 2-Digit and 4-Digit Quotients

Use Activity
Workbook page 33.

► Practice

Divide.

6. 4)868

7. 6)5,142

8. 3)4,395

9. 4)332

10. 7)1,617

11. 7)939

12. 2)4,276

13. 6)2,576

14. 7)441

15. 9)3,735

16. 7)406

17. 3)9,954

Show your work on your paper or in your journal.

▶ Division Word Problems

Solve.

18. What is the length of a rectangle with an area of 756 square centimeters and a width of 4 centimeters?

	?
4	756

19. At a county fair, there are 7 booths that sell raffle tickets. In one day, 4,592 tickets were sold. Each booth sold the same number of tickets. How many tickets did each booth sell?

20. One part of a city football stadium has 5,688 seats. The seats are arranged in 9 sections. Each section has the same number of seats. How many seats are in each section?

21. An art museum has a total of 475 paintings hanging in 5 different viewing rooms. If each room has the same number of paintings, how many paintings are in each room?

22. A parking garage can hold a total of 762 cars. The same number of cars can park on each floor. There are 6 floors. How many cars can park on each floor?

Discuss 2-Digit and 4-Digit Quotients

▶ The Digit-by-Digit Method

1. Suppose Judith wants to divide 948 by 4. She knows how to use the Place Value Sections Method and the Expanded Notation Method, but she doesn't want to write all the zeros.

Place Value Sections Method

$$
\begin{array}{c}
\quad\ \ 200 + \quad 30 + \quad 7\ = 237 \\
4\ \begin{array}{|c|c|c|}
\hline
948 & 148 & 28 \\
-\,800 & -\,120 & -\,28 \\
\hline
\end{array} \\
\ \ \ 148 \qquad\ \ 28 \qquad\ \ 0
\end{array}
$$

Expanded Notation Method

$$
\begin{array}{r}
7 \\
30 \\
200 \\
\hline
4\overline{)948} \\
-800 \\
\hline
148 \\
-120 \\
\hline
28 \\
-28 \\
\hline
0
\end{array} \Bigg]\ 237
$$

Judith thinks: I'll look at the place values in decreasing order. I'll imagine zeros in the other places, but I don't need to think about them until I'm ready to divide in that place.

Step 1: Look at the greatest place value first. Divide the hundreds. Then subtract.

9 hundreds ÷ 4 = 2 hundreds

$$
\begin{array}{r}
2 \\
4\overline{)948} \\
-8 \\
\hline
1
\end{array}
$$

Step 2: Bring down the 4. Divide the tens. Then subtract.

14 tens ÷ 4 = 3 tens

$$
\begin{array}{r}
23 \\
4\overline{)948} \\
-8\downarrow \\
\hline
14 \\
-12 \\
\hline
2
\end{array}
$$

Step 3: Bring down the 8. Divide the ones. Then subtract.

28 ones ÷ 4 = 7 ones

$$
\begin{array}{r}
237 \\
4\overline{)948} \\
-8 \\
\hline
14 \\
-12\downarrow \\
\hline
28 \\
-28 \\
\hline
0
\end{array}
$$

▶ What's the Error?

Dear Math Students,

Here is a division problem I tried to solve.

$$
\begin{array}{r}
5{,}796 \\
3\overline{)1{,}738} \\
-15 \\
\hline
23 \\
-21 \\
\hline
28 \\
-27 \\
\hline
18 \\
-18 \\
\hline
0
\end{array}
$$

Is my answer correct? If not, please help me understand why it is wrong.

Thank you,
Puzzled Penguin

2. Write a response to Puzzled Penguin.

Solve. Use the Digit-by-Digit Method.

3. $4\overline{)3{,}036}$ **4.** $7\overline{)5{,}292}$ **5.** $6\overline{)853}$

Use Activity
Workbook page 34.

► Practice

Divide.

6. $5\overline{)965}$ 7. $8\overline{)128}$ 8. $8\overline{)928}$

9. $3\overline{)716}$ 10. $4\overline{)4,596}$ 11. $4\overline{)982}$

12. $3\overline{)6,342}$ 13. $8\overline{)578}$ 14. $5\overline{)1,155}$

15. $6\overline{)3,336}$ 16. $7\overline{)672}$ 17. $3\overline{)4,152}$

▶ Solve Division Problems

Write an equation to represent the problem.
Then, solve.

18. What is the length of a rectangle with an area of 528 square centimeters and a width of 6 centimeters?

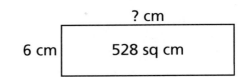

19. A cookbook features 414 recipes. There are 3 recipes on each page. How many pages are in the cookbook?

20. A bus travels its route around a city once a day for 5 days. At the end of the 5th day, the bus had traveled 435 miles. How many miles did the bus travel each day?

21. Ms. Tyler places a container of marbles at each table of 6 students. The students are told to share the marbles equally with the students at their table. If there are 714 marbles in the container, how many marbles should each student get?

22. Sam's Used Bookstore is organizing their books on display shelves. They have 976 books and want 8 books displayed on each shelf. How many shelves will the books fill?

Digit-by-Digit Method

► Compare Methods

Ellie, José, and Wanda each use their favorite method to solve 1,194 ÷ 5. Discuss the methods.

Ellie's Place Value Sections Method	José's Expanded Notation Method	Wanda's Digit-by-Digit Method

Ellie's Place Value Sections Method:

$$200 + 30 + 8 = 238\ R4$$

$$5\ \begin{array}{|c|c|c|}\hline 1{,}194 & 194 & 44 \\ -1{,}000 & -150 & -40 \\ \hline 194 & 44 & 4 \\ \end{array}$$

José's Expanded Notation Method:

$$\left.\begin{array}{r} 8 \\ 30 \\ 200 \end{array}\right\} 238\ R4$$

$$5\overline{)1{,}194}$$
$$-\,1{,}000$$
$$\overline{194}$$
$$-\,150$$
$$\overline{44}$$
$$-\,40$$
$$\overline{4}$$

Wanda's Digit-by-Digit Method:

$$\begin{array}{r} 238\ R4 \\ 5\overline{)1{,}194} \\ -1\,0 \\ \hline 19 \\ -15 \\ \hline 44 \\ -40 \\ \hline 4 \end{array}$$

Use any method to solve.

1. 3,248 ÷ 5 = ▩

2. 5,847 ÷ 6 = ▩

Solve. Use any method.

3. $5\overline{)8{,}435}$

4. $3\overline{)2{,}604}$

5. $4\overline{)6{,}738}$

6. $5\overline{)9{,}714}$

▶ Division Practice

Use any method to solve.

7. $6\overline{)2,238}$ 8. $5\overline{)2,431}$ 9. $7\overline{)2,198}$ 10. $8\overline{)2,512}$

11. $4\overline{)5,027}$ 12. $5\overline{)5,624}$ 13. $9\overline{)3,631}$ 14. $6\overline{)6,305}$

▶ What's the Error?

Dear Math Students,

This is a problem from my math homework. My teacher says my answer is not correct, but I can't figure out what I did wrong. Can you help me find and fix my mistake?

$$
\begin{array}{r}
7,069 \text{ R2} \\
5\overline{)3,847} \\
-35 \\
\hline
34 \\
-30 \\
\hline
47 \\
-45 \\
\hline
2
\end{array}
$$

Your Friend,
Puzzled Penguin

15. Write a response to Puzzled Penguin.

▶ Practice Division

Use any method to solve.

1. 8)960

2. 4)632

3. 7)809

4. 5)736

5. 4)3,068

6. 3)6,206

7. 2)6,476

8. 6)8,825

▶ Solve Division Word Problems

Solve.

Show your work on your paper or in your journal.

9. A helper in the school store suggests selling notebooks in packages of 4. How many packages of 4 can be made from 192 notebooks?

10. Another helper suggests selling notebooks in packages of 6. How many packages of 6 can be made from 192 notebooks?

11. The store will sell packages of notebooks for $3.00 each.

   a. Which would be a better deal for students, packages of 4 or packages of 6?

   b. Which package size would make more money for the store?

▶ Solve Division Word Problems (continued)

Another helper in the school store suggests making packages of 7 or 8 notebooks.

12. How many packages of 7 notebooks can be made from 896 notebooks?

13. How many packages of 8 notebooks can be made from 896 notebooks?

14. The store will sell packages of notebooks for $6.00 each.

   a. Would you rather buy a package with 7 notebooks or a package with 8 notebooks? Explain.

   b. Would packages of 7 notebooks or packages of 8 notebooks make more money for the store? Explain.

15. The students at Walnut Street School collected 2,790 cans for a recycling center. Each student brought in 5 cans. How many students attend the school?

16. A cube can be made from 6 square cards that are each the same size. How many cubes can be made out of 7,254 cards?

17. There are 5,896 beads in a barrel at a factory. These beads will be sold in packets of 4. How many full packets can be made from the beads in the barrel?

▶ What's the Error?

Dear Math Students,

The Puzzled Penguin started to solve this division problem and realized there was a problem. Some friends suggested different ways to fix it.

Your friend,
Puzzled Penguin

$$\begin{array}{r} 7 \\ 4\overline{)3,476} \\ -28 \\ \hline 6 \end{array}$$

Jacob suggested that Puzzled Penguin erase the 7 and write 8 in its place. Puzzled Penguin would also need to erase the calculations and do them over. $$\begin{array}{r} 8 \\ 4\overline{)3,476} \\ -32 \\ \hline 2 \end{array}$$	Fred told Puzzled Penguin to cross out the 7 and write 8 above it. The next step would be to subtract one more 4. $$\begin{array}{r} 8 \\ \cancel{7} \\ 4\overline{)3,476} \\ -28 \\ \hline 6 \\ -4 \end{array}$$
Amad showed Puzzled Penguin how to use the Expanded Notation Method and just keep going. $$\begin{array}{r} 100 \\ 700 \\ 4\overline{)3,476} \\ -2,800 \\ \hline 676 \\ -400 \\ \hline 276 \end{array}$$	Kris showed Puzzled Penguin how, with the Place Value Sections Method, another section can be added. $$\begin{array}{c|c|c} & 700 \;+ & 100 \\ \hline 4 & 3,476 & 676 \\ & -2,800 & -400 \\ \hline & 676 & 276 \end{array}$$

1. What was Puzzled Penguin's problem?

2. Discuss the solutions above. Which friend was right?

► Zeros in Quotients

Solve.

3. 6)1,842

4. 8)5,125

5. 4)4,152

6. 5)9,522

7. 3)7,531

8. 2)4,018

9. 4)8,200

10. 7)9,102

11. Cameron has a collection of 436 miniature cars that he displays on 4 shelves in a bookcase. If the cars are divided equally among the shelves, how many cars are on each shelf?

Show your work on your paper or in your journal.

12. The Tropical Tour Company has 2,380 brochures to distribute equally among its 7 resort hotels. How many brochures will each hotel receive?

13. A factory packs 8,440 bottles of water in boxes each day. If each box contains 8 bottles, how many full boxes of water can the factory pack in one day?

Just-Under Quotient Digits

▶ Check Quotients With Rounding and Estimation

Rounding and estimating can be used to check answers. Review your rounding skills, and then apply what you know to division problems.

Use rounding and estimating to decide whether each quotient makes sense.

1. 18 R2
    3)56

2. 92 R3
    5)463

3. 928
    6)5,568

4. 129 R4
    7)907

▶ Practice Dividing and Estimating

Solve, using any method. Then check your answer by rounding and estimating.

5. 3)29

6. 6)34

7. 7)59

8. 3)72

9. 6)83

10. 7)88

11. 7)628

12. 8)683

13. 9)717

14. 7)805

15. 8)869

16. 9)914

17. 6)1,723

18. 2)2,986

19. 7)8,574

20. 6)4,652

21. 2)5,235

22. 7)7,310

▶ Estimate or Exact Answer

Some problems require an exact answer. Others require
an estimate only.

Exact Answer If a problem asks for an exact answer, then you will have to do the calculation. **Example:** The school cafeteria prepares 3,210 lunches each week. The same numbers of lunches are prepared 5 days each week. How many lunches are prepared each day? Discuss why you think this problem requires an exact answer.	**Estimate** If a problem asks for a close answer and uses *about, approximately, almost,* or *nearly,* then you can estimate. **Example:** Milo has to read a 229-page book. He has 8 days to finish it. About how many pages should he read each day? Discuss why an estimate, and not an exact answer, is appropriate.

**Decide whether you need an exact answer or an estimate.
Then find the answer.**

23. Sam bought a board that was
72 inches long to make
bookshelves. He wants to cut the
board into three equal pieces and
use each one for a shelf. How long
will each shelf be?

24. Carl's mother baked 62 mini
muffins for his class. There are
18 people in Sam's class, including
the teacher. About how many mini
muffins should each person get?

25. Each 24-inch shelf can hold about
10 books. Approximately how
many inches wide is each book?

26. Malcom wants to buy 3 concert
tickets. Each ticket costs $45.
How much money will he need?

▶ Different Kinds of Remainders

Remainders in division have different meanings, depending upon the type of problem you solve.

$$\begin{array}{r} 2\text{ R}1 \\ 4\overline{)9} \\ -8 \\ \hline 1 \end{array}$$

The same numeric solution shown at the right works for the following five problems. Discuss why the remainder means something different in each problem.

A. **The remainder is not part of the question.** Thomas has one 9-foot pine board. He needs to make 4-foot shelves for his books. How many shelves can he cut?

B. **The remainder causes the answer to be rounded up.** Nine students are going on a field trip. Parents have offered to drive. If each parent can drive 4 students, how many parents need to drive?

C. **The remainder is a fractional part of the answer.** One Monday Kim brought 9 apples to school. She shared them equally among herself and 3 friends. How many apples did each person get?

D. **The remainder is a decimal part of the answer.** Raul bought 4 toy cars for $9.00. Each car costs the same amount. How much did each car cost?

E. **The remainder is the only part needed to answer the question.** Nine students have signed up to run a relay race. If each relay team can have 4 runners, how many students cannot run in the race?

Show your work
on your paper or
in your journal.

▶ Discuss Real World Division Problems

Solve. Then discuss the meaning of the remainder.

1. Maddie tried to divide 160 stickers equally among herself and 5 friends. There were some stickers left over, so she kept them. How many stickers did Maddie get?

2. Kendra bought a bag of 200 cheese crackers for her class. If each student gets 7 crackers, how many students are there? How many crackers are left over?

3. Jerry bought shelves to hold the 132 DVDs in his collection. Each shelf can fit 8 DVDs. How many full shelves will Jerry have?

4. Racheed had 87 pennies. He divided them equally among his 4 sisters. How many pennies did Racheed have left after he gave his sisters their shares?

5. Mara wants to buy some new pencil boxes for her pencil collection. She has 47 pencils. If each pencil box holds 9 pencils, how many pencil boxes does Mara need to buy?

6. Henry's coin bank holds only nickels. Henry takes $4.42 to the bank to exchange for nickels only. How many nickels will he get from the bank?

> **Show your work on your paper or in your journal.**

► Mixed One-Step Word Problems

The fourth- and fifth-grade classes at Jackson Elementary
School held a Just-for-Fun Winter Carnival. All of the students
in the school were invited.

**Discuss what operation you need to use to solve each
problem. Then solve the problem.**

1. Two students from each fourth-
and fifth-grade class were on the
planning committee. If Jackson
School has 14 fourth- and fifth-
grade classes in all, how many
students planned the carnival?

2. To advertise the carnival, students
decorated 4 hallway bulletin boards.
They started with 2,025 pieces of
colored paper. When they finished,
they had 9 pieces left. How many
pieces of paper did they use?

3. The parents ordered pizzas to serve
at the carnival. Each pizza was cut
into 8 slices. How many pizzas had
to be ordered so that 1,319 people
could each have one slice?

4. There were 825 students signed up
to run in timed races. If exactly 6
students ran in each race, how many
races were there?

5. At the raffle booth, 364 fourth-
graders each bought one ticket to
win a new school supply set. Only
8 fifth-graders each bought a ticket.
How many students bought raffle
tickets altogether?

6. Altogether, 1,263 students were
enrolled in the first through fifth
grades at Jackson School. On the
day of the carnival, 9 students were
absent. How many students could
have participated in the carnival
activities?

Show your work on your paper or in your journal.

▶ Mixed Multistep Word Problems

Solve these problems about Pine Street School's Olympic Games.

7. At the start of the games, 193 fourth-graders signed up to play in three events. Eighty-seven played in the first event. The rest of the students were evenly divided between the second and third events. How many students played in the third event?

8. Three teams stacked paper cups into pyramids. Each team had 176 cups to use. Team 1 used exactly half of their cups. Team 2 used four times as many cups as Team 3. Team 3 used 32 cups. Which team stacked the most cups?

9. The Parents' Club provided 357 celery sticks, 676 carrot sticks, and 488 apple slices. If each student was given 3 snack pieces, how many students got a snack?

10. Seventy-five first-graders and 84 second-graders skipped around the gym. After a while, only 8 students were still skipping. How many students had stopped skipping?

11. A team from each school had 250 foam balls and a bucket. The Jackson team dunked 6 fewer balls than the Pine Street team. The Pine Street team dunked all but 8 of their balls. How many balls did the two teams dunk in all?

12. When the day was over, everybody had earned at least 1 medal, and 32 students each got 2 medals. In all, 194 each of gold, silver, and bronze medals were given out. How many students played in the games?

Mixed Problem Solving

► Math and Amusement Parks

There are many things to do at an Amusement Park: ride the rides, play some games, try new foods. Many people like to ride roller coasters while at the Amusement Park.

The tallest roller coaster in the world is 456 feet tall and is located in Jackson, New Jersey. In fact, the top three tallest roller coasters in the world are in the United States.

The fourth and fifth grade classes went on a field trip to the Amusement Park.

1. There are 58 fourth grade students who are in line to ride the Loop-the-Loop roller coaster. Each roller coaster car holds 4 people. How many roller coaster cars are needed so they all can ride the roller coaster once?

Show your work on your paper or in your journal.

2. There are 41 fifth grade students who are in line to ride the Mile Long wooden roller coaster. Each roller coaster car holds 6 people. How many students will be in a roller coaster car that is not full?

▶ More Amusement Park Fun

After riding the roller coasters, the fourth and fifth grade classes spend the rest of the day getting lunch, going shopping, and riding the rest of the rides at the Amusement Park.

Solve.

3. There are 27 students in Evan's group. Each student decides to get a kids meal for lunch at the food stand. If each kids meal is $7, how much did the students spend in lunch altogether?

> *Show your work on your paper or in your journal.*

4. Thirty-one students are in line to ride the Ferris wheel. Four students are needed to fill each Ferris wheel car. How many Ferris wheel cars will be full?

5. In the souvenir shop, a worker opens a box of posters. The posters in the box are bundled in groups of 8. There are a total of 2,864 posters in a box. How many bundles of posters are in the box?

Focus on Mathematical Practices

Use the Activity Workbook Unit Test on pages 35–36.

VOCABULARY
dividend
divisor
remainder
quotient

▶ **Vocabulary**

Choose the best term from the box.

1. A _____ is an answer to a division problem. (Lesson 3-1)

2. The number 7 is the _____ in the division problem 548 ÷ 7. (Lesson 3-1)

3. In the division problem 548 ÷ 7, the number 548 is the _____. (Lesson 3-1)

▶ **Concepts and Skills**

4. List the three methods suggested in this Unit for solving division problems. Which division method would you use to solve 728 ÷ 6? Explain why you chose that method and how you would use it to solve the problem. (Lessons 3-2, 3-3, 3-4, 3-5)

5. Explain why you need to write a zero in the tens place of the quotient when you divide 829 by 4. (Lesson 3-7)

6. For what types of real world division problems might you use the quotient alone? When might you use only the remainder? (Lesson 3-9)

Use rounding and estimation to decide whether each quotient makes sense. (Lesson 3-8)

7. $6\overline{)297}$ 49 R3

8. $4\overline{)3,256}$ 814

9. $8\overline{)4,229}$ 528 R5

Use any method to solve. (Lessons 3-1, 3-2, 3-3, 3-4, 3-5, 3-6, 3-7)

10. 4)716

11. 9)959

12. 3)6,243

13. 7)940

14. 4)2,203

15. 7)8,659

16. 5)7,534

17. 6)9,915

▶ Problem Solving

Solve.

18. There are 185 students going to a museum. Each van can hold 9 students. How many vans of 9 students will there be? How many students will ride in a van that is not full? Lesson 3-9

19. Joshua pulls 52 loads of sand on his wagon to make a play area. He pulls 21 pounds of sand on each load. How many pounds of sand does Joshua use to make a play area? Lesson 3-10

20. **Extended Response** Kayla and her father baked 256 banana nut muffins and 298 chocolate chip muffins to sell at their family restaurant. They plan to place the muffins in boxes that hold 6 muffins each. What is the greatest number of boxes that can be filled with muffins? Explain how you found your answer. Lessons 3-9, 3-10

Family Letter

Dear Family,

In Unit 4 of Math Expressions, your child will apply the skills he or she has learned about operations with whole numbers while solving real world problems involving addition, subtraction, multiplication, and division.

Your child will simplify and evaluate expressions. Parentheses will be introduced to show which operation should be done first. The symbols "=" and "≠" will be used to show whether numbers and expressions are equal.

Other topics of study in this unit include situation and solution equations for addition and subtraction, as well as multiplication and division. Your child will use situation equations to represent real world problems and solution equations to solve the problems. This method of representing a problem is particularly helpful when the problems contain greater numbers and students cannot solve mentally.

Your child will also solve multiplication and addition comparison problems and compare these types of problems identifying what is the same or different.

Share with your family the Family Letter on Activity Workbook page 37.

Addition Comparison	Multiplication Comparison
Angela is 14 years old. She is 4 years older than Damarcus. How old is Damarcus?	Shawn colored 5 pages in a coloring book. Anja colored 4 times as many pages as Shawn colored. How many pages did Anja color?

Students learn that in the addition problem they are adding 4, while in the multiplication problem, they are multiplying by 4.

Your child will apply this knowledge to solve word problems using all four operations and involving one or more steps.

Finally, your child will find factor pairs for whole numbers and generate and analyze numerical and geometric patterns.

If you have any questions or comments, please call or write to me.

Sincerely,
Your child's teacher

COMMON CORE

This unit includes the Common Core Standards for Mathematical Content for Operations and Algebraic Thinking 4.OA.1, 4.OA.2, 4.OA.3, 4.OA.4, 4.OA.5, Number and Operations in Base Ten 4.NBT.4, 4.NBT.5, 4.NBT.6, Measurement and Data 4.MD.2, and all Mathematical Practices.

Estimada familia:

En la Unidad 4 de Math Expressions, su hijo aplicará las destrezas relacionadas con operaciones de números enteros que ha adquirido, resolviendo problemas cotidianos que involucran suma, resta, multiplicación y división.

Su hijo simplificará y evaluará expresiones. Se introducirán los paréntesis como una forma de mostrar cuál operación deberá completarse primero. Los signos "=" y "≠" se usarán para mostrar si los números o las expresiones son iguales o no.

Otros temas de estudio en esta unidad incluyen ecuaciones de situación y de solución para la suma y resta, así como para la multiplicación y división. Su hijo usará ecuaciones de situación para representar problemas de la vida cotidiana y ecuaciones de solución para resolver esos problemas. Este método para representar problemas es particularmente útil cuando los problemas involucran números grandes y los estudiantes no pueden resolverlos mentalmente.

Su hijo también resolverá problemas de comparación de multiplicación y suma, y comparará este tipo de problemas para identificar las semejanzas y diferencias.

Comparación de suma	Comparación de multiplicación
Ángela tiene 14 años. Ella es 4 años mayor que Damarcus. ¿Cuántos años tiene Damarcus?	Shawn coloreó 5 páginas de un libro. Ana coloreó 4 veces ese número de páginas. ¿Cuántas páginas coloreó Ana?

Muestra a tu familia la Carta a la familia de la página 38 del Cuaderno de actividades y trabajo.

Los estudiantes aprenderán que en el problema de suma están sumando 4, mientras que en el problema de multiplicación, están multiplicando por 4.

Su hijo aplicará estos conocimientos para resolver problemas de uno o más pasos usando las cuatro operaciones.

Finalmente, su hijo hallará pares de factores para números enteros y generará y analizará patrones numéricos y geométricos.

Si tiene alguna pregunta por favor comuníquese conmigo.

Atentamente,
El maestro de su niño

COMMON CORE

Esta unidad incluye los Common Core Standards for Mathematical Content for Operations and Algebraic Thinking 4.OA.1, 4.OA.2, 4.OA.3, 4.OA.4, 4.OA.5, Number and Operations in Base Ten 4.NBT.4, 4.NBT.5, 4.NBT.6, Measurement and Data 4.MD.2, and all Mathematical Practices.

Properties and Algebraic Notation

VOCABULARY
expression
equation
simplify
term

▶ Properties and Algebraic Notation

An **expression** is one or more numbers, variables, or numbers and variables with one or more operations. Examples: 4 $6x$ $6x - 5$ $7 + 4$	An **equation** is a statement that two expressions are equal. It has an equal sign. Examples: $40 + 25 = 65$ $(16 \div 4) - 3 = 1$

We **simplify** an expression or equation by performing operations to combine like **terms**.

Use the Identity Property to simplify each expression.

1. $n + 5n =$ ▪

2. $17t + t =$ ▪

3. $x + 245x =$ ▪

4. $9e - e =$ ▪

5. $8c + c + c =$ ▪

6. $(5z - z) - z =$ ▪

Solve.

7. $30 \div (35 \div 7) =$ ▪

8. $(72 \div 9) \div 4 =$ ▪

9. $80 \div (32 \div 8) =$ ▪

10. $13 - (9 - 1) =$ ▪

11. $(600 - 400) - 10 =$ ▪

12. $100 - (26 - 6) =$ ▪

Use properties to find the value of ☐ or a.

13. $49 + 17 = \boxed{} + 49$

☐ = ▪

14. $(a \cdot 2) \cdot 3 = 4 \cdot (2 \cdot 3)$

$a =$ ▪

15. $\boxed{} \cdot 6 = 6 \cdot 8$

☐ = ▪

16. $6 \cdot (40 + a) = (6 \cdot 40) + (6 \cdot 5)$

$a =$ ▪

17. $(\boxed{} \cdot 5) + (\boxed{} \cdot 9) = 7 \cdot (5 + 9)$

☐ = ▪

18. $29 + 8 = \boxed{} + 29$ ⟶ Is $\boxed{} = 4 + 2$ or $4 \cdot 2$?

19. $a \cdot 14 = 14 \cdot 15$ ⟶ Is $a = 5 \cdot 3$ or $5 + 3$?

20. $60 + 10 = \boxed{} + 60$ ⟶ Is $\boxed{} = 2 + 5$ or $2 \cdot 5$?

VOCABULARY
evaluate

▶ Parentheses in Equations

Solve.

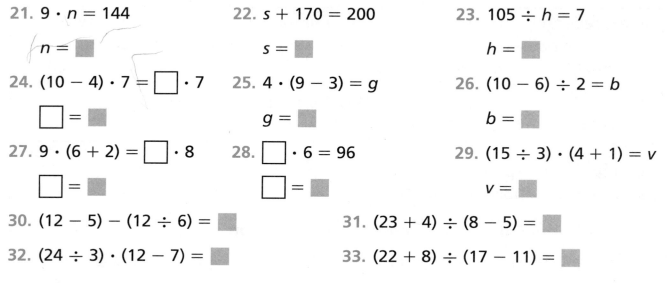

21. $9 \cdot n = 144$

 $n = $ ▪

22. $s + 170 = 200$

 $s = $ ▪

23. $105 \div h = 7$

 $h = $ ▪

24. $(10 - 4) \cdot 7 = \square \cdot 7$

 $\square = $ ▪

25. $4 \cdot (9 - 3) = g$

 $g = $ ▪

26. $(10 - 6) \div 2 = b$

 $b = $ ▪

27. $9 \cdot (6 + 2) = \square \cdot 8$

 $\square = $ ▪

28. $\square \cdot 6 = 96$

 $\square = $ ▪

29. $(15 \div 3) \cdot (4 + 1) = v$

 $v = $ ▪

30. $(12 - 5) - (12 \div 6) = $ ▪

31. $(23 + 4) \div (8 - 5) = $ ▪

32. $(24 \div 3) \cdot (12 - 7) = $ ▪

33. $(22 + 8) \div (17 - 11) = $ ▪

▶ Substitute a Value

To **evaluate** an expression or equation:

1) Substitute the value of each letter.

2) Then simplify the expression by performing the operations.

Evaluate each expression.

34. $a = 4$

 $19 - (a + 6)$

35. $a = 10$

 $(80 \div a) - 5$

36. $b = 3$

 $(8 \div 4) \cdot (7 - b)$

37. $b = 7$

 $21 \div (b - 4)$

38. $b = 11$

 $(b + 9) \div (7 - 2)$

39. $c = 8$

 $(20 - 10) + (7 + c)$

40. $x = 9$

 $16 \cdot (13 - x)$

41. $d = 3$

 $(24 \div 3) \cdot (d + 7)$

42. $d = 0$

 $(63 \div 7) \cdot d$

Properties and Algebraic Notation

VOCABULARY
sum
difference

▶ Discuss the = and ≠ Signs

An equation is made up of two equal quantities or expressions. An equal sign (=) is used to show that the two sides of the equation are equal.

$5 = 3 + 2$ $3 + 2 = 5$ $5 = 5$ $3 + 2 = 2 + 3$ $7 - 2 = 1 + 1 + 3$

The "is not equal to" sign (≠) shows that two quantities are not equal.

$4 \neq 3 + 2$ $5 \neq 3 - 1$ $5 \neq 4$ $3 - 2 \neq 1 + 3$ $3 + 2 \neq 1 + 1 + 2$

An equation can have one or more numbers or letters on each side of the equal sign. A **sum** or **difference** can be written on either side of the equal sign.

1. Use the = sign to write four equations. Vary how many numbers you have on each side of your equations.

2. Use the ≠ sign to write four "is not equal to" statements. Vary how many numbers you have on each side of your statements.

Write = or ≠ to make each statement true.

3. $5 + 2 + 6$ ▊ $6 + 7$ 4. 80 ▊ $60 - 20$ 5. 70 ▊ $40 + 30$

6. $18 - 4 + 11$ ▊ 3 7. 50 ▊ $55 - (10 + 5)$ 8. $21 + 6 - 3$ ▊ $26 - 4 + 2$

Use Activity
Workbook page 39.

▶ Discuss Inverse Operations

When you add, you put two groups together. When you subtract, you find an unknown addend or take away one group from another. Addition and subtraction are inverse operations. They undo each other.

Addends are numbers that are added to make a sum. You can find two addends for a sum by breaking apart the number.

Total (Sum)

Addend

Addend

A break-apart drawing can help you find all eight related addition and subtraction equations for two addends.

Total (Sum)
81
/ \
72   9
Addend   Addend

$81 = 72 + 9$ $72 + 9 = 81$

$81 = 9 + 72$ $9 + 72 = 81$

$72 = 81 - 9$ $81 - 9 = 72$

$9 = 81 - 72$ $81 - 72 = 9$

9. Which equations show the Commutative Property?

10. What is the total in each equation? Where is the total in a subtraction equation?

Solve each equation.

11. $50 = 30 + p$

$p = \blacksquare$

12. $q + 20 = 60$

$q = \blacksquare$

13. $90 - v = 50$

$v = \blacksquare$

14. Write the eight related addition and subtraction equations for the break-apart drawing.

56
/ \
48   8

VOCABULARY
situation equation
solution equation

▶ Write Equations to Solve Problems

A **situation equation** shows the structure of the information in a problem. A **solution equation** shows the operation that can be used to solve a problem.

Show your work on your paper or in your journal.

Write an equation to solve the problem. Draw a model if you need to.

15. In a collection of 2,152 coins, 628 coins are pennies. How many coins are not pennies?

16. Susanna took $3,050 out of her bank account. Now she has $11,605 left in the account. How much money was in Susanna's account to start?

17. In the month of May, Movieland rented 563 action movies and 452 comedy movies. How many action and comedy movies in all did Movieland rent in May?

▶ Practice Solving Problems

Write an equation to solve the problem. Draw a model if you need to.

18. The workers at a factory made 3,250 pink balloons in the morning. There were 5,975 pink balloons at the factory at the end of the day. How many pink balloons did the factory workers make in the afternoon?

Show your work
on your paper or
in your journal.

► Practice Solving Problems (continued)

19. Terrence is planning a 760-mile trip. He travels 323 miles the first two days. How many miles does Terrence have left to travel on this trip?

20. There were some people at the football stadium early last Sunday, and then 5,427 more people arrived. Then there were 79,852 people at the stadium. How many people arrived early?

► What's the Error?

Dear Math Students,

The problem shown below was part of my homework assignment.

Mrs. Nason has a collection of 1,845 stamps. She bought some more stamps. Now she has 2,270 stamps. How many stamps did Mrs. Nason buy?

To solve the problem, I wrote this equation:
$s - 1,845 = 2,270$. I solved the equation and wrote $s = 4,115$.

My teacher says that my answer is not correct. Can you help me understand what I did wrong and explain how to find the correct answer?

Your Friend,
Puzzled Penguin

21. Write a response to Puzzled Penguin.

Situation and Solution Equations for Addition and Subtraction

▶ Discuss Inverse Operations

Multiplication and division are inverse operations. They undo each other.

A **factor pair** for a number is a pair of whole numbers whose product is that number. For example, a factor pair for 15 is 3 and 5. A rectangle model is a diagram that shows a factor pair and the product.

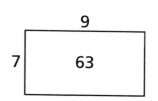

1. Which numbers in the rectangle model above are the factors? Where are the factors located?

2. Which number is the product? Where is the product located?

A rectangle model can you help you find all eight related multiplication and division equations for two factors. You can write these equations for the rectangle model above.

$$63 = 7 \times 9 \qquad\qquad 7 \times 9 = 63$$
$$63 = 9 \times 7 \qquad\qquad 9 \times 7 = 63$$
$$7 = 63 \div 9 \qquad\qquad 63 \div 9 = 7$$
$$9 = 63 \div 7 \qquad\qquad 63 \div 7 = 9$$

3. Write the eight related multiplication and division equations for the rectangle model below.

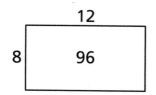

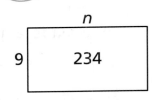

Show your work on your paper or in your journal.

▶ Write Equations to Solve Problems

Read the problem and answer the questions.

	n
9	234

4. Brenda planted 234 trees on her farm. The farm has 9 rows of trees. How many trees are in each row?

   a. The number of trees on the farm is known. Write the number.

   b. The number of rows of trees is known. Write the number.

   c. The number of trees in each row is unknown. Use the letter *n* to represent the number of trees in each row. Write a situation equation to solve the problem.

   d. Write a solution equation.

   e. Solve your equation.

Write an equation to solve the problem. Draw a model if you need to.

5. Evan is starting a cycling program. He will ride 315 miles each month for the next 6 months. How many miles does he plan to ride in all?

6. Suki has 152 stickers to place in a sticker album. How many pages will Suki fill with stickers if each page in the album holds 8 stickers?

7. Al bought a wall pattern with 27 rows of 28 squares. How many squares are in the wall pattern?

Situation and Solution Equations for Multiplication and Division

VOCABULARY
compare
comparison bars

▶ Discuss Comparison Problems

To prepare for a family gathering, Sara and Ryan made soup. Sara made 2 quarts. Ryan made 6 quarts.

You can **compare** amounts, using multiplication and division.

Let *r* equal the number of quarts Ryan made.
Let *s* equal the number of quarts Sara made.

Ryan made 3 times as many quarts as Sara.

$$r = 3 \cdot s, \; r = 3s, \text{ or } s = r \div 3$$

Ryan (r)	2	2	2	6
Sarah (s)	2	2	2	

Solve.

Natasha made 12 quarts of soup. Manuel made 3 quarts.

1. Draw **comparison bars** to show the amount of soup each person made.

2. _____ made 4 times as many quarts as _____.

3. Write a multiplication equation that compares the amounts.

4. Write a division equation that compares the amounts.

5. Multiplication is the putting together of equal groups. How can this idea be used to explain why a *times as many* comparing situation is multiplication?

Show your work on your paper or in your journal.

▶ Share Solutions

**Write an equation to solve each problem.
Draw a model if you need to.**

6. There are 24 students in the science club. There are 2 times as many students in the drama club. How many students are in the drama club?

   a. Draw comparison bars to compare the numbers of students in each club.

   b. Write an equation to solve the problem.

7. There are 180 pennies in Miguel's coin collection and that is 5 times as many as the number of quarters in his coin collection. How many quarters does Miguel have?

8. Fred has 72 football cards and Scott has 6 football cards. How many times as many football cards does Fred have as Scott has?

9. Audrey has 1,263 centimeters of fabric, and that is 3 times as much fabric as she needs to make some curtains. How many centimeters of fabric does Audrey need to make the curtains?

Multiplication Comparisons

▶ Discuss Comparison Situations

In Lesson 4-4, you learned about multiplication and division **comparison situations**. You can also compare by using addition and subtraction. You can find *how much more* or *how much less* one amount is than another.

The amount more or less is called the difference. In some problems, the difference is not given. You have to find it. In other problems, the lesser or the greater amount is not given.

Mai has 9 apples and 12 plums.

- How many more plums than apples does Mai have?

Plums | 12

- How many fewer apples than plums does Mai have?

Apples | 9 | *d*

Comparison bars can help us show which is more. We show the difference in an oval.

Draw comparison bars for each problem. Write and solve an equation. Discuss other equations you could use.

1. A nursery has 70 rose bushes and 50 tea-tree bushes. How many fewer tea-tree bushes than rose bushes are at the nursery?

2. Dan wants to plant 30 trees. He has dug 21 holes. How many more holes does Dan need to dig?

Show your work
on your paper or
in your journal.

▶ **Share Solutions**

Draw comparison bars for each problem.
Write and solve an equation.

3. Kyle and Mackenzie are playing a computer
   game. Kyle scored 7,628 points. Mackenzie
   scored 2,085 fewer points than Kyle. How
   many points did Mackenzie score?

4. The school fair fundraiser made $632 more
   from baked goods than from games. The
   school fair made $935 from games. How
   much money did the school fair make from
   baked goods?

5. A college football stadium in Michigan seats
   109,901 people. A college football stadium in
   Louisiana seats 92,542 people. How many
   fewer people does the stadium in Louisiana
   seat than the stadium in Michigan?

6. The soccer team drilled for 150 minutes last
   week. The team drilled for 30 minutes more
   than it scrimmaged. For how long did the
   team scrimmage?

Discuss Comparison Problems

Show your work on your paper or in your journal.

► Solve Comparison Problems

For each problem, draw a model and write *addition* or *multiplication* to identify the type of comparison. Then write and solve an equation to solve the problem.

7. Nick and Liz both collect marbles. Liz has 4 times as many marbles as Nick. If Nick has 240 marbles, how many marbles does Liz have?

   Type of comparison:

   Equation and answer:

8. Samantha has 145 fewer songs on her portable media player than Luke has on his portable media player. If Samantha has 583 songs, how many songs does Luke have?

   Type of comparison:

   Equation and answer:

9. A large bookstore sold 19,813 books on Saturday and 22,964 books on Sunday. How many fewer books did the bookstore sell on Saturday than on Sunday?

   Type of comparison:

   Equation and answer:

10. Last weekend, Mr. Morgan rode his bike 3 miles. This weekend, he rode his bike 21 miles. How many times as many miles did Mr. Morgan ride his bike this weekend as last weekend?

    Type of comparison:

    Equation and answer:

Show your work on your paper or in your journal.

► Practice

Write and solve an equation to solve each problem.
Draw comparison bars when needed.

11. On the last day of school, 100 more students wore shorts than wore jeans. If 130 students wore jeans, how many students wore shorts?

12. Matthew completed a puzzle with 90 pieces. Wendy completed a puzzle with 5 times as many pieces. How many pieces are in Wendy's puzzle?

13. There were 19,748 adults at a baseball game. There were 5,136 fewer children at the baseball game than there were adults. How many children were at the baseball game?

► What's the Error?

Dear Math Students,

I was asked to find the number of stamps that Amanda has if her friend Jesse has 81 stamps and that is 9 times as many stamps as Amanda has.

To solve the problem, I wrote this equation: $81 \times 9 = s$. I solved the equation and wrote $s = 729$. My teacher says that my answer is not correct. Can you help me understand what I did wrong?

Your friend,
Puzzled Penguin

14. Write a response to Puzzled Penguin.

Discuss Comparison Problems

▶ Use a Pictograph

A **pictograph** is a graph that uses pictures or symbols to represent data. This pictograph shows how many books 5 students checked out of a library in one year.

Books Checked Out of Library

Student	
Najee	📖 📖
Tariq	📖 📖 📖 📖 📖 📖
Celine	📖 📖 📖 📖 📖 📖 📖 📖
Jamarcus	📖 📖 📖
Brooke	📖 📖 📖 📖

📖 = 5 books

Use the pictograph to solve.

1. Write an addition equation and a subtraction equation that compare the number of books Tariq checked out (t) to the number of books Jamarcus checked out (j).

2. Write a multiplication equation and a division equation that compare the number of books Najee checked out (n) to the number of books Celine checked out (c).

3. Celine checked out twice as many books as which student?

4. Which student checked out 30 fewer books than Celine?

5. The number of books Dawson checked out is not shown. If Jamarcus checked out 10 more books than Dawson, how many books did Dawson check out?

Show your work on your paper or in your journal.

▶ Use a Bar Graph

The bar graph below shows the number of home runs hit by five members of a baseball team.

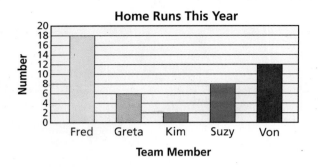

Use the bar graph to solve.

6. Write an addition equation and a subtraction equation that compare the number of home runs Suzy hit (s) to the number of home runs Kim hit (k).

7. Write a multiplication equation and a division equation that compare the number of home runs Greta hit (g) to the number of runs Fred hit (f).

8. How many more home runs did Von hit than Greta?

9. Which player hit 10 fewer home runs than Von?

10. This year, Fred hit 2 times as many home runs as he hit last year. How many home runs did Fred hit last year?

11. Math Journal Write a sentence about the graph that contains the words *times as many*.

Graphs and Comparison Problems

4-7

Class Activity

▶ Discuss the Steps of the Problem

Sometimes you will need to work through more than one step to solve a problem. The steps can be shown in one or more equations.

Solve.

1. At Parkes Elementary School, there are 6 fourth-grade classes with 17 students in each class. On Friday, 23 fourth-graders brought lunch from home and the rest of the students bought lunch in the cafeteria. How many fourth-graders bought lunch in the cafeteria on Friday?

2. Solve the problem again by finishing Tommy's and Lucy's methods. Then discuss how the two methods are alike and how they are different.

Tommy's Method	Lucy's Method
Write an equation for each step.	Write an equation for the whole problem.
Find the total number of students who are in fourth grade. $6 \times 17 = $ ▨ Subtract the number of students who brought lunch from home. $102 - 23 = $ ▨	Let $n = $ the number of students who bought lunch. Students in each fourth grade class. Students who brought lunch from home. $6 \quad \times \quad ▨ \quad - \quad ▨ \quad = n$ ▨ $= n$

3. Use an equation to solve. Discuss the steps you used.

Susan buys 16 packages of hot dogs for a barbecue. Each package contains 12 hot dogs. Hot-dog buns are sold in packages of 8. How many packages of hot-dog buns does Susan need to buy so she has one bun for each hot dog?

Show your work on your paper or in your journal.

► Share Solutions

Use an equation to solve.

4. Admission to the theme park is $32 for each adult. A group of 5 adults and 1 child pays $182 to enter the theme park. How much is a child's ticket to the theme park?

5. Kenny collects CDs and DVDs. He has a total of 208 CDs. He also has 8 shelves with 24 DVDs on each shelf. How many more CDs does Kenny have than DVDs?

6. Carla plants 14 tomato plants. Her gardening book says that each plant should grow 12 tomatoes. She plans to divide the tomatoes equally among herself and 7 friends. How many tomatoes would each person get?

7. Alex and his family go on a roadtrip. On the first day, they drive 228 miles. On the second day, they drive 279 miles. Their destination is 1,043 miles away. How many miles do they have left to drive to reach their destination?

8. A public library has more than 50,000 books. There are 249 science books and 321 technology books. Mary sorts the science and technology books on shelves with 6 books on each shelf. How many shelves will Mary fill with science and technology books?

Use Activity
Workbook page 40.

▶ **Discuss the Steps**

1. Mr. Stills makes bags of school supplies for the 9 students in his class. He has 108 pencils and 72 erasers. He puts the same number of pencils and the same number of erasers into each bag. How many more pencils than erasers are in each bag of school supplies?

Solve the problem by finishing Nicole's and David's methods. Discuss what is alike and what is different about the methods.

Nicole's Method

Write an equation for each step.

Divide to find the number of pencils that Mr. Stills puts in each bag of school supplies.
$$108 \div 9 = \boxed{}$$

Divide to find the number of erasers that Mr. Stills puts in each bag of school supplies.
$$72 \div 9 = \boxed{}$$

Subtract the number of erasers in each bag from the number of pencils in each bag.
$$12 - 8 = \boxed{}$$

There are ____ more pencils than erasers in each bag of school supplies.

David's Method

Write an equation for the whole problem.

Let p = how many more pencils than erasers are in each bag of school supplies

The number of pencils in each bag of school supplies.   The number of erasers in each bag of school supplies.

$$\boxed{} \div 9 - \boxed{} \div 9 = p$$
$$12 - 8 = p$$
$$\boxed{} = p$$

There are ____ more pencils than erasers in each bag of school supplies.

> Use Activity
> Workbook page 41.

▶ Discuss the Steps (continued)

2. John is selling bags of popcorn for a school fundraiser. So far, John has sold 45 bags of popcorn for $5 each. His goal is to earn $300 for the school fundraiser. How many more bags of popcorn must John sell to reach his goal?

Solve the problem by writing an equation for each step. Then solve the problem by writing one equation for the whole problem.

Write an equation for each step.

Multiply to find how much money John has earned so far selling popcorn.

$$\boxed{} \times \ \$5 \ = \ \$\boxed{}$$

Subtract to find how much money John has left to earn to reach his goal.

$$\$300 \ - \ \$\boxed{} \ = \$\boxed{}$$

Divide to find the number of bags of popcorn John must sell to reach his goal.

$$\$75 \ \div \ \$5 \ = \ \boxed{}$$

John must sell ___\boxed{}___ more bags of popcorn to reach his goal.

Write an equation for the whole problem.

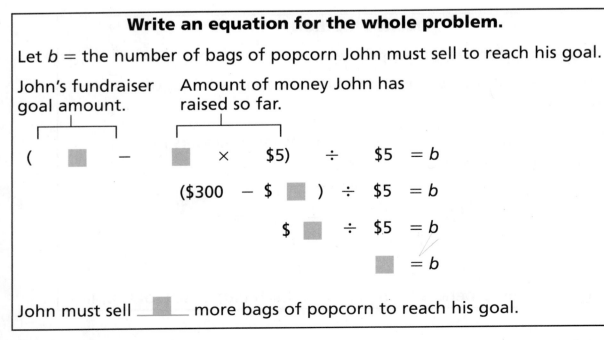

Let b = the number of bags of popcorn John must sell to reach his goal.

John's fundraiser goal amount.   Amount of money John has raised so far.

$$(\ \boxed{} \ - \ \boxed{} \ \times \ \$5) \ \div \ \$5 \ = b$$

$$(\$300 \ - \ \$\boxed{}\ ) \ \div \ \$5 \ = b$$

$$\$\boxed{} \ \div \ \$5 \ = b$$

$$\boxed{} \ = b$$

John must sell ___\boxed{}___ more bags of popcorn to reach his goal.

Solve Multistep Problems

Show your work
on your paper or
in your journal.

► Multistep Word Problems

Use an equation to solve.

3. Sara bought some bags of beads. Each bag had
   9 beads and cost $2. Sara used the beads to make
   18 necklaces, each with 25 beads. How much money
   did Sara pay for the beads for all of the necklaces that
   she made?

4. There are 5 fourth-grade classes going on a field trip.
   Two of the classes have 16 students each and 3 of the
   classes have 17 students each. They are travelling in
   vans that hold 9 students each. How many vans must
   they have to transport all the students?

5. A movie theater has 13 screens. On weekends, each
   screen shows a movie 7 times in one day. On weekdays,
   each screen shows a movie 5 times in one day. How
   many more showings are there on Saturdays than on
   Tuesdays?

6. Justin goes to the store and buys 3 T-shirts for
   $14 each. He also buys 2 pairs of jeans for $23 each.
   He gives the cashier $100. How much change does
   Justin receive?

7. Terrence has 24 model cars arranged in equal rows of
   6 model cars. Natalie has 18 model cars arranged
   in equal rows of 3 model cars. How many rows of
   model cars in all do they have?

▶ What's the Error?

Dear Math Students,

My friend and I are planning a hike. We will hike from point *A* to point *B*, which is a distance of 28 miles. Then we will hike from Point *B* to Point *C*, which is a distance of 34 miles. We will walk 7 miles each day for 8 days. We are trying to figure out how many miles we need to walk on the ninth day to reach Point *C*.

I wrote and solved this equation.

$28 + 34 - 7 \times 8 = t$

$62 - 7 \times 8 = t$

$55 \times 8 = t$

$440 = t$

This answer doesn't make sense. Did I do something wrong? What do you think?

Your friend,
Puzzled Penguin

8. Write a response to Puzzled Penguin.

Show your work on your paper or in your journal.

▶ Discuss Multistep Word Problems

Use equations to solve.

1. Eli reads 6 pages in a book each night. Shelby reads 8 pages each night. How many pages altogether will Eli and Shelby read in one week?

2. Min Soo is ordering 5 pizzas for a party. Each pizza will be cut into 8 slices. Three pizzas will have multiple toppings, and the others will be plain cheese. How many slices of plain cheese pizza is Min Soo ordering for the party?

3. Jasmine and Mori each received the same number of party favor bags at a friend's party. Each bag contained 8 favors. If Jasmine and Mori received a total of 48 favors, how many party favor bags did they each receive?

4. In art class, Ernesto made some fruit bowls for his mother and brother. Nine apples can be placed in each bowl. Ernesto's brother placed 18 apples in the bowls he was given, and Ernesto's mother placed 36 apples in the bowls she was given. How many fruit bowls did Ernesto make?

5. On Tuesday, a bicycle shop employee replaced all of the tires on 6 bicycles. On Wednesday, all of the tires on 5 tricycles were replaced. What is the total number of tires that were replaced on those days?

Show your work on your paper or in your journal.

▶ Solve Multistep Word Problems

Use equations to solve.

6. Mrs. Luong bought 9 trees for $40 each. She paid for her purchase with four $100 bills. How much change did she receive?

7. Chan Hee is carrying a box that weighs 37 pounds. In the box are five containers of equal weight, and a book that weighs 2 pounds. What is the weight of each container?

8. A pet shop is home to 6 cats, 10 birds, 3 dogs, and 18 tropical fish. Altogether, how many legs do those pets have?

9. Dan has 7 fish in his aquarium. Marilyn has 4 times as many fish in her aquarium. How many fish do Dan and Marilyn have altogether?

10. Write a problem that is solved using more than one step. Then show how to solve the problem.

Practice with Multistep Problems

Use Activity
Workbook page 42.

▶ Find Factor Pairs

A factor pair for a number is two whole numbers whose product is that number. For example, 2 and 5 is a factor pair for 10.

1. Draw arrays to show all the factor pairs for 12 on the grid below. The array for 1 and 12 is shown.

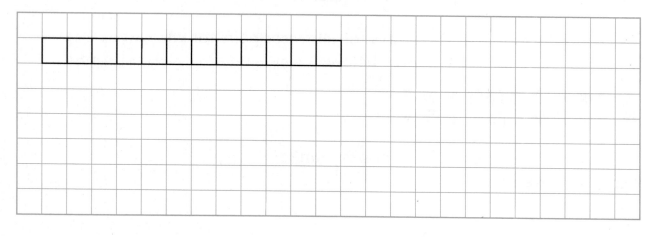

2. List all the factor pairs for 12.

Use the table to find all the factors pairs for each number.

3. 32

1	32
2	

4. 44

1	44

5. 100

1	100

List all the factor pairs for each number.

6. 29

7. 63

▶ Identify Prime and Composite Numbers

A number greater than 1 that has 1 and itself as its only factor pair is a **prime number**. Some prime numbers are 2, 5, 11, and 23.

A number greater than 1 that has more than one factor pair is a **composite number**. Some composite numbers are 4, 12, 25, and 100.

The number 1 is neither prime nor composite.

8. Use counters to model the arrays for all factor pairs for 24. The array for 2 and 12 is shown below.

9. Is 24 a *prime number* or a *composite number*? Explain your answer.

Write whether each number is *prime* or *composite*.

10. 99

11. 72

12. 31

13. 45

14. 19

15. 88

16. 67

17. 100

18. 53

19. Is 2 the only even prime number? Explain.

▶ Factors and Multiples

A **multiple** of a number is a product of that number and a counting number.

20. What are the first five multiples of 4? Explain your method.

21. Write the first ten multiples of 8.

22. Is 54 a multiple of 6? Explain how you know.

23. Is 6 a factor of 40? Explain how you know.

24. What are the first five multiples of 9? Explain your method.

25. What are the factors of 63?

26. Is 63 a multiple of each factor that you listed for Exercise 25? Explain how you know.

▶ Practice With Factors and Multiples

Tell whether 7 is a factor of each number. Write *yes* or *no*.

27. 7   28. 84   29. 93   30. 49

Tell whether each number is a multiple of 9. Write *yes* or *no*.

31. 27   32. 30   33. 81   34. 99

Use a pattern to find the unknown multiples.

35. $3 \times 11 = 33$

   $4 \times 11 = 44$

   $5 \times 11 = \blacksquare$

   $6 \times 11 = \blacksquare$

   $7 \times 11 = \blacksquare$

36. $5 \times 6 = 30$

   $6 \times 6 = \blacksquare$

   $7 \times 6 = \blacksquare$

   $8 \times 6 = \blacksquare$

   $9 \times 6 = \blacksquare$

Use the rule to complete the pattern.

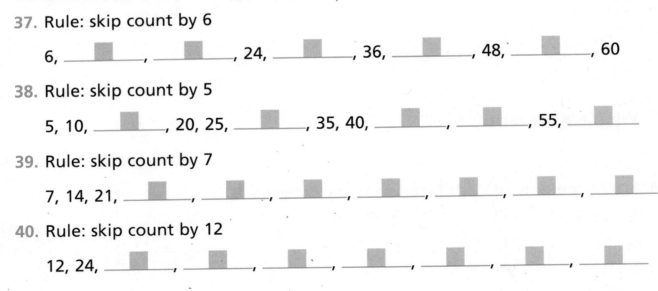

37. Rule: skip count by 6

   6, _____, _____, 24, _____, 36, _____, 48, _____, 60

38. Rule: skip count by 5

   5, 10, _____, 20, 25, _____, 35, 40, _____, _____, 55, _____

39. Rule: skip count by 7

   7, 14, 21, _____, _____, _____, _____, _____, _____, _____

40. Rule: skip count by 12

   12, 24, _____, _____, _____, _____, _____, _____, _____

▶ Numerical Patterns

A **pattern** is a sequence that can be described by a rule.

Use the rule to find the next three terms in the pattern.

1. 22, 24, 26, 28, 30, …
   Rule: add 2

2. 5, 10, 20, 40, …
   Rule: multiply by 2

3. 1, 3, 9, 27, …
   Rule: multiply by 3

4. 2, 9, 16, 23, 30, …
   Rule: add 7

Use the rule to find the first ten terms in the pattern.

5. First term: 9   Rule: add 5

6. First term: 10   Rule: add 60

▶ Real World Applications

Solve.

7. Amy lives in the twentieth house on Elm Street. The first house on Elm Street is numbered 3. The second is 6. The third is 9. The fourth is 12. If this pattern continues, what is Amy's house number likely to be?

House	1st	2nd	3rd	4th	20th
Number	3	6	9	12	

8. Theo runs 5 miles every morning. He tracks his progress on a chart to log how many miles he has run in all. How many miles will Theo write on the 100th day?

Day	1	2	3	4	5	100
Miles	5	10	15	20	25	

▶ Extend Patterns

9. What are the repeating terms of the pattern?

10. What will be the tenth term in the pattern?

11. What will be the fifteenth term in the pattern?

▶ Growing Patterns

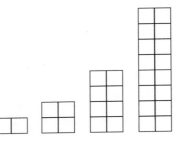

12. How does each figure in the pattern change from one term to the next?

13. Describe the number of squares in the next term in the pattern?

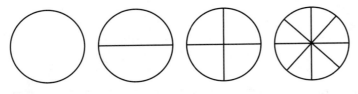

14. How does each figure in the pattern change from one term to the next?

15. How many equal parts will be in the seventh term?

▶ Math and Pottery

Pottery are objects that are first shaped of wet clay and then hardened by baking. Four steps are needed to make a pottery product: preparing the clay mixture, shaping the clay, decorating and glazing the product, and baking the product. Pottery includes products such as works of art, dinnerware, vases, and other household items. Some of the places you can find pottery include art studios, crafts shows, pottery stores, and most households.

Write an equation to solve.

Show your work on your paper or in your journal.

1. A small pottery store has 9 boxes full of pottery items. The boxes weigh 765 pounds in all. How much does each box weigh?

2. Julio and Myra had a pottery stand at the annual craft fair. They sold some of their pottery at the original price of $13 each and made $780. Later in the day, they decreased the price of each item by $4 and sold 20 more items. How much money did they make in all that day?

Image Credits: ©Image Source/Getty Images

Show your work on your paper or in your journal.

Write an equation to solve.

3. Last month, Mr. Smith bought 65 small cans of paint for his pottery shop. This month he bought 3 times as many small cans of paint. How many small cans of paint did he buy this month?

4. The employees at a pottery warehouse are packing boxes of vases to be delivered by truck. They packed 824 small vases in boxes that each hold 8 vases. They also packed 296 large vases in boxes that each hold 4 vases. How many boxes did the workers pack in all?

5. Last year, there were 3,875 different pottery items for sale at a large crafts show. This year, there were 1,260 fewer pottery items for sale at the crafts show. How many pottery items were for sale at the crafts show this year?

Solve.

6. Isabella saw a pottery design that she liked at a crafts store. She wants to copy the design and paint it on a pot she is making. Part of the design is shown below.

a. What shape should Isabella paint next to continue the design's pattern?

b. What will be the fourteenth term in Isabella's design?

Focus on Mathematical Practices

Use the Activity
Workbook Unit Test on
pages 43–46.

VOCABULARY
composite number
prime number
situation equation
solution equation

▶ Vocabulary

Choose the best term from the box.

1. A _____ shows the operation that can be used to solve a problem. (Lessons 4-2, 4-3)

2. A number greater than 1 that has 1 and itself as its only factor pair is a _____ (Lesson 4-10)

3. A _____ shows the structure of the information in a problem. (Lessons 4-2, 4-3)

▶ Concepts and Skills

4. Explain how the equation for *4 is 2 more than 2* is different from the equation for *4 is 2 times as many as 2.* (Lessons 4-4, 4-5, 4-6)

5. Explain how you could use rectangles and circles to show the following pattern: A B B A B B A B B. (Lesson 4-11)

6. Dori wrote this problem: Mrs. Ramos has 1,352 stamps. She buys some more stamps. Now she has 1,943 stamps. How many stamps did she buy? Explain why the situation equation $1,352 + s = 1,943$ represents Dori's problem. (Lesson 4-2)

Solve for ☐ **or** *n*. (Lesson 4-1)

7. $(18 - 9) \cdot 3 = \boxed{} \cdot 3$

    ☐ = ▆

8. $(35 + 50) - (25 \div 5) = n$

    $n = $ ▆

List all factor pairs for each number. (Lesson 4-10)

9. 47

10. 28

Write whether each number is *prime* or *composite*. (Lesson 4-10)

11. 98

12. 61

Tell whether each number is a multiple of 7. Write *yes* or *no*. (Lesson 4-10)

13. 36

14. 84

Use the rule to find the next three terms in the pattern. (Lesson 4-11)

15. 6, 12, 24, 48, ...
    Rule: multiply by 2

16. 55, 95, 135, 175, ...
    Rule: add 40

17. 4, 12, 36, 108, ...
    Rule: multiply by 3

Describe the next term of each pattern. (Lesson 4-11)

18.

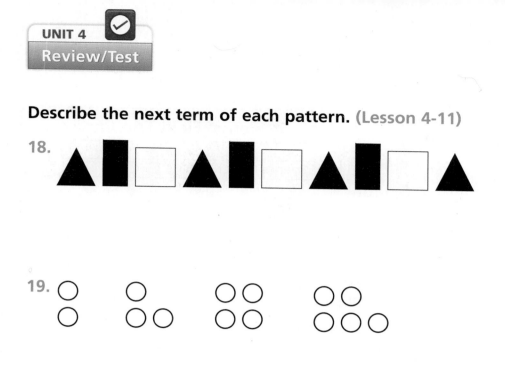

19.

► Problem Solving

For Problems 20–21, write an equation to solve the problem. (Lessons 4-2, 4-3)

20. The Appalachian Trail is a hiking trail that runs from Maine to Georgia and is approximately 2,160 miles long. Suppose the Andersons want to hike 9 miles per day along an 864-mile section of the trail from New York to Georgia. On how many days will the Andersons hike 9 miles?

21. The library had a large collection of books. Then the librarian ordered 2,200 more books. Now there are 13,327 books. How many books did the library have at the start?

For Problems 22–23, use the pictograph.
Write an equation to solve each
comparison problem. (Lessons 4-4, 4-5, 4-6)

22. How many fewer students voted for
    the zoo than voted for the aquarium?

Students' Field Trip Choices	
Zoo	☺ ☺ ☺
Science Center	☺ ☺ ☺ ☺ ☺ ☺
Aquarium	☺ ☺ ☺ ☺ ☺ ☺ ☺
Art Museum	☺ ☺

☺ = 4 votes

23. How many times as many students voted for the
    science center as voted for the art museum?

For Problems 24–25, use an equation to solve.
(Lessons 4-7, 4-8, 4-9)

24. Rita and Cody sold refreshments at the football
    game. They sold 6 sandwiches, 8 bags of popcorn,
    and 20 bottles of water. The sandwiches cost
    $5 each. The bags of popcorn cost $2 each.
    The bottles of water cost $1 each. How much
    money in all did Rita and Cody make?

25. **Extended Response** A bakery had 2 trays with
    28 muffins on each tray. The bakery had 4 trays
    of cupcakes with 12 cupcakes on each tray.
    On Monday, the bakery sold 12 cupcakes.

    a. How many muffins and cupcakes were left in all?
       Explain.

    b. How can you determine if your answer is reasonable?

Reference Tables

Table of Measures

Metric	Customary

Length/Area

Metric	Customary
1,000 millimeters (mm) = 1 meter (m)	1 foot (ft) = 12 inches (in.)
100 centimeters (cm) = 1 meter	1 yard (yd) = 36 inches
10 decimeters (dm) = 1 meter	1 yard = 3 feet
1 dekameter (dam) = 10 meters	1 mile (mi) = 5,280 feet
1 hectometer (hm) = 100 meters	1 mile = 1,760 yards
1 kilometer (km) = 1,000 meters	

Liquid Volume

Metric	Customary
1,000 milliliters (mL) = 1 liter (L)	6 teaspoons (tsp) = 1 fluid ounce (fl oz)
100 centiliters (cL) = 1 liter	2 tablespoons (tbsp) = 1 fluid ounce
10 deciliters (dL) = 1 liter	1 cup (c) = 8 fluid ounces
1 dekaliter (daL) = 10 liters	1 pint (pt) = 2 cups
1 hectoliter (hL) = 100 liters	1 quart (qt) = 2 pints
1 kiloliter (kL) = 1,000 liters	1 gallon (gal) = 4 quarts

Mass / Weight

Mass	Weight
1,000 milligrams (mg) = 1 gram (g)	1 pound (lb) = 16 ounces
100 centigrams (cg) = 1 gram	1 ton (T) = 2,000 pounds
10 decigrams (dg) = 1 gram	
1 dekagram (dag) = 10 grams	
1 hectogram (hg) = 100 grams	
1 kilogram (kg) = 1,000 grams	
1 metric ton = 1,000 kilograms	

Table of Units of Time

Time

1 minute (min) = 60 seconds (sec)	1 year = 365 days
1 hour (hr) = 60 minutes	1 leap year = 366 days
1 day = 24 hours	1 decade = 10 years
1 week (wk) = 7 days	1 century = 100 years
1 month, about 30 days	1 millennium = 1,000 years
1 year (yr) = 12 months (mo) or about 52 weeks	

Table of Formulas

Perimeter

Polygon

P = sum of the lengths of the sides

Rectangle

$P = 2(l + w)$ or $P = 2l + 2w$

Square

$P = 4s$

Area

Rectangle

$A = lw$ or $A = bh$

Square

$A = s \cdot s$

Properties of Operations

Associative Property of Addition

$$(a + b) + c = a + (b + c) \qquad (2 + 5) + 3 = 2 + (5 + 3)$$

Commutative Property of Addition

$$a + b = b + a \qquad 4 + 6 = 6 + 4$$

Addition Identity Property of 0

$$a + 0 = 0 + a = a \qquad 3 + 0 = 0 + 3 = 3$$

Associative Property of Multiplication

$$(a \cdot b) \cdot c = a \cdot (b \cdot c) \qquad (3 \cdot 5) \cdot 7 = 3 \cdot (5 \cdot 7)$$

Commutative Property of Multiplication

$$a \cdot b = b \cdot a \qquad 6 \cdot 3 = 3 \cdot 6$$

Multiplicative Identity Property of 1

$$a \cdot 1 = 1 \cdot a = a \qquad 8 \cdot 1 = 1 \cdot 8 = 8$$

Distributive Property of Multiplication over Addition

$$a \cdot (b + c) = (a \cdot b) + (a \cdot c) \qquad 2 \cdot (4 + 3) = (2 \cdot 4) + (2 \cdot 3)$$

Problem Types

Addition and Subtraction Problem Types

	Result Unknown	Change Unknown	Start Unknown
Add to	A glass contained $\frac{3}{4}$ cup of orange juice. Then $\frac{1}{4}$ cup of pineapple juice was added. How much juice is in the glass now? Situation and solution equation: [1] $\frac{3}{4} + \frac{1}{4} = c$	A glass contained $\frac{3}{4}$ cup of orange juice. Then some pineapple juice was added. Now the glass contains 1 cup of juice. How much pineapple juice was added? Situation equation: $\frac{3}{4} + c = 1$ Solution equation: $c = 1 - \frac{3}{4}$	A glass contained some orange juice. Then $\frac{1}{4}$ cup of pineapple juice was added. Now the glass contains 1 cup of juice. How much orange juice was in the glass to start? Situation equation $c + \frac{1}{4} = 1$ Solution equation: $c = 1 - \frac{1}{4}$
Take from	Micah had a ribbon $\frac{5}{6}$ yard long. He cut off a piece $\frac{1}{6}$ yard long. What is the length of the ribbon that is left? Situation and solution equation: $\frac{5}{6} - \frac{1}{6} = r$	Micah had a ribbon $\frac{5}{6}$ yard long. He cut off a piece. Now the ribbon is $\frac{4}{6}$ yard long. What is the length of the ribbon he cut off? Situation equation: $\frac{5}{6} - r = \frac{4}{6}$ Solution equation: $r = \frac{5}{6} - \frac{4}{6}$	Micah had a ribbon. He cut off a piece $\frac{1}{6}$ yard long. Now the ribbon is $\frac{4}{6}$ yard long. What was the length of the ribbon he started with? Situation equation: $r - \frac{1}{6} = \frac{4}{6}$ Solution equation: $r = \frac{4}{6} + \frac{1}{6}$

[1] A situation equation represents the structure (action) in the problem situation. A solution equation shows the operation used to find the answer.

	Total Unknown	Addend Unknown	Other Addend Unknown
Put Together/ Take Apart	A baker combines $1\frac{2}{3}$ cups of white flour and $\frac{2}{3}$ cup of wheat flour. How much flour is this altogether?	Of the $2\frac{1}{3}$ cups of flour a baker uses, $1\frac{2}{3}$ cups are white flour. The rest is wheat flour. How much wheat flour does the baker use?	A baker uses $2\frac{1}{3}$ cups of flour. Some is white flour and $\frac{2}{3}$ cup is wheat flour. How much white flour does the baker use?

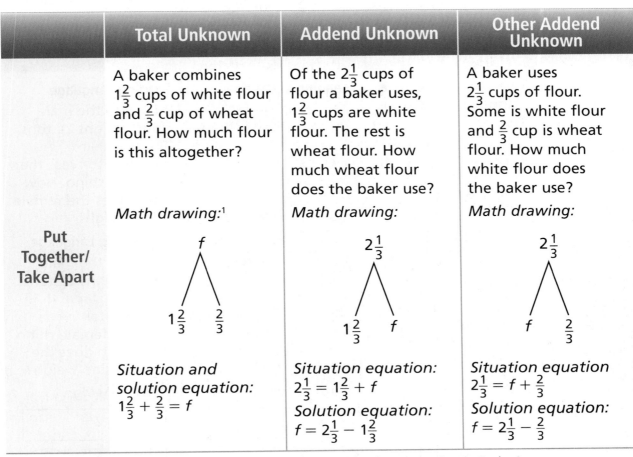

	Total Unknown	Addend Unknown	Other Addend Unknown
	Math drawing:[1]	*Math drawing:*	*Math drawing:*
	Situation and solution equation: $1\frac{2}{3} + \frac{2}{3} = f$	*Situation equation:* $2\frac{1}{3} = 1\frac{2}{3} + f$ *Solution equation:* $f = 2\frac{1}{3} - 1\frac{2}{3}$	*Situation equation* $2\frac{1}{3} = f + \frac{2}{3}$ *Solution equation:* $f = 2\frac{1}{3} - \frac{2}{3}$

[1]These math drawings are called math mountains in Grades 1–3 and break apart drawings in Grades 4 and 5.

Problem Types continued

Addition and Subtraction Problem Types (continued)

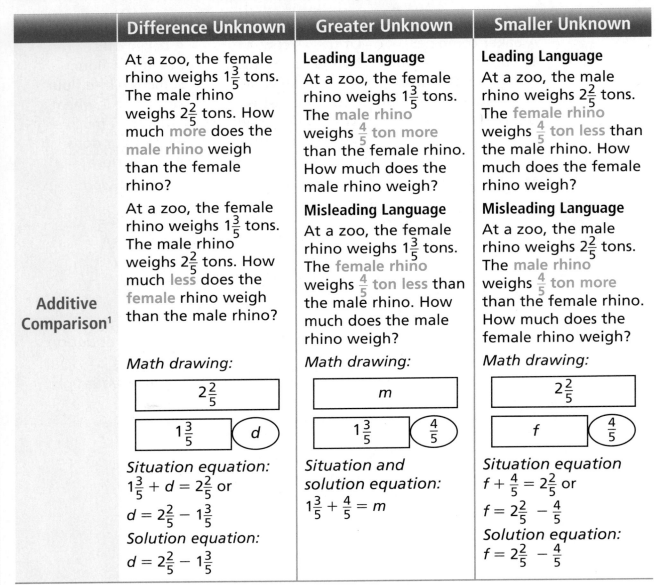

	Difference Unknown	Greater Unknown	Smaller Unknown
Additive Comparison[1]	At a zoo, the female rhino weighs $1\frac{3}{5}$ tons. The male rhino weighs $2\frac{2}{5}$ tons. How much more does the male rhino weigh than the female rhino?	**Leading Language** At a zoo, the female rhino weighs $1\frac{3}{5}$ tons. The male rhino weighs $\frac{4}{5}$ ton more than the female rhino. How much does the male rhino weigh?	**Leading Language** At a zoo, the male rhino weighs $2\frac{2}{5}$ tons. The female rhino weighs $\frac{4}{5}$ ton less than the male rhino. How much does the female rhino weigh?
	At a zoo, the female rhino weighs $1\frac{3}{5}$ tons. The male rhino weighs $2\frac{2}{5}$ tons. How much less does the female rhino weigh than the male rhino?	**Misleading Language** At a zoo, the female rhino weighs $1\frac{3}{5}$ tons. The female rhino weighs $\frac{4}{5}$ ton less than the male rhino. How much does the male rhino weigh?	**Misleading Language** At a zoo, the male rhino weighs $2\frac{2}{5}$ tons. The male rhino weighs $\frac{4}{5}$ ton more than the female rhino. How much does the female rhino weigh?
	Math drawing: $2\frac{2}{5}$ / $1\frac{3}{5}$ d	*Math drawing:* m / $1\frac{3}{5}$ $\frac{4}{5}$	*Math drawing:* $2\frac{2}{5}$ / f $\frac{4}{5}$
	Situation equation: $1\frac{3}{5} + d = 2\frac{2}{5}$ or $d = 2\frac{2}{5} - 1\frac{3}{5}$ *Solution equation:* $d = 2\frac{2}{5} - 1\frac{3}{5}$	*Situation and solution equation:* $1\frac{3}{5} + \frac{4}{5} = m$	*Situation equation* $f + \frac{4}{5} = 2\frac{2}{5}$ or $f = 2\frac{2}{5} - \frac{4}{5}$ *Solution equation:* $f = 2\frac{2}{5} - \frac{4}{5}$

[1]A comparison sentence can always be said in two ways. One way uses *more*, and the other uses *fewer* or *less*. Misleading language suggests the wrong operation. For example, it says *the female rhino weighs* $\frac{4}{5}$ *ton less than the male*, but you have to add $\frac{4}{5}$ ton to the female's weight to get the male's weight.

Multiplication and Division Problem Types

	Unknown Product	Group Size Unknown	Number of Groups Unknown
Equal Groups	A teacher bought 10 boxes of pencils. There are 20 pencils in each box. How many pencils did the teacher buy? *Situation and solution equation:* $p = 10 \cdot 20$	A teacher bought 10 boxes of pencils. She bought 200 pencils in all. How many pencils are in each box? *Situation equation:* $10 \cdot n = 200$ *Solution equation:* $n = 200 \div 10$	A teacher bought boxes of 20 pencils. She bought 200 pencils in all. How many boxes of pencils did she buy? *Situation equation* $b \cdot 20 = 200$ *Solution equation:* $b = 200 \div 20$

	Unknown Product	Unknown Factor	Unknown Factor
Arrays[1]	An auditorium has 60 rows with 30 seats in each row. How many seats are in the auditorium? *Math drawing:* (rectangle: 30 across top, 60 on left side, s inside) *Situation and solution equation:* $s = 60 \cdot 30$	An auditorium has 60 rows with the same number of seats in each row. There are 1,800 seats in all. How many seats are in each row? *Math drawing:* (rectangle: n across top, 60 on left side, 1,800 inside) *Situation equation:* $60 \cdot n = 1,800$ *Solution equation:* $n = 1,800 \div 60$	The 1,800 seats in an auditorium are arranged in rows of 30. How many rows of seats are there? *Math drawing:* (rectangle: 30 across top, r on left side, 1,800 inside) *Situation equation* $r \cdot 30 = 1,800$ *Solution equation:* $r = 1,800 \div 30$

[1]We use rectangle models for both array and area problems in Grades 4 and 5 because the numbers in the problems are too large to represent with arrays.

Problem Types (continued)

Multiplication and Division Problem Types (continued)

	Unknown Product	Unknown Factor	Unknown Factor
Area	Sophie's backyard is 80 feet long and 40 feet wide. What is the area of Sophie's backyard? *Math drawing:* 80 / 40 / A *Situation and solution equation:* $A = 80 \cdot 40$	Sophie's backyard has an area of 3,200 square feet. The length of the yard is 80 feet. What is the width of the yard? *Math drawing:* 80 / w / 3,200 *Situation equation:* $80 \cdot w = 3{,}200$ *Solution equation:* $w = 3{,}200 \div 80$	Sophie's backyard has an area of 3,200 square feet. The width of the yard is 40 feet. What is the length of the yard? *Math drawing:* l / 40 / 3,200 *Situation equation* $l \cdot 40 = 3{,}200$ *Solution equation:* $l = 3{,}200 \div 40$
Multiplicative Comparison	**Whole Number Multiplier** Sam has 4 times as many marbles as Brady has. Brady has 70 marbles. How many marbles does Sam have? *Math drawing:* s: 70 | 70 | 70 | 70 b: 70 *Situation and solution equation:* $s = 4 \cdot 70$	**Whole Number Multiplier** Sam has 4 times as many marbles as Brady has. Sam has 280 marbles. How many marbles does Brady have? *Math drawing:* 280 s: b: *Situation equation:* $4 \cdot b = 280$ *Solution equation:* $b = 280 \div 4$	**Whole Number Multiplier** Sam has 280 marbles. Brady has 70 marbles. The number of marbles Sam has is how many times the number Brady has? *Math drawing:* 280 s: 70 | 70 | 70 | 70 b: 70 *Situation equation* $m \cdot 70 = 280$ *Solution equation:* $m = 280 \div 70$

Vocabulary Activities

► Word Review PAIRS

Work with a partner. Choose a word from a current unit or a review word from a previous unit. Use the word to complete one of the activities listed on the right. Then ask your partner if they have any edits to your work or questions about what you described. Repeat, having your partner choose a word.

Activities

► Give the meaning in words or gestures.

► Use the word in the sentence.

► Give another word that is related to the word in some way and explain the relationship.

► Crossword Puzzle PAIRS OR INDIVIDUALS

Create a crossword puzzle similar to the example below. Use vocabulary words from the unit. You can add other related words, too. Challenge your partner to solve the puzzle.

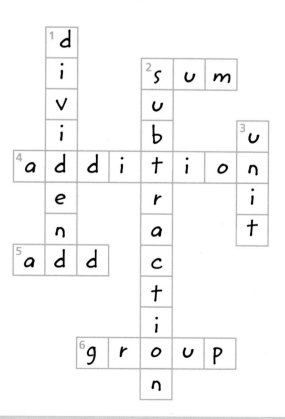

Across

2. The answer to an addition problem

4. _____ and subtraction are inverse operations.

5. To put amounts together

6. When you trade 10 ones for 1 ten, you _____.

Down

1. The number to be divided in a division problem

2. The operation that you can use to find out how much more one number is than another.

3. A fraction with a numerator of 1 is a _____ fraction.

Vocabulary Activities (continued)

▶ Word Wall   PAIRS OR SMALL GROUPS

With your teacher's permission, start a word wall in your classroom. As you work through each lesson, put the math vocabulary words on index cards and place them on the word wall. You can work with a partner or a small group choosing a word and giving the definition.

▶ Word Web   INDIVIDUALS

Make a word web for a word or words you do not understand in a unit. Fill in the web with words or phrases that are related to the vocabulary word.

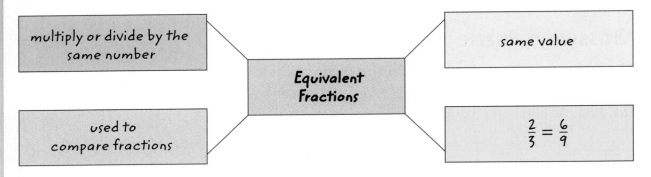

multiply or divide by the same number		same value
	Equivalent Fractions	
used to compare fractions		$\frac{2}{3} = \frac{6}{9}$

▶ Alphabet Challenge   PAIRS OR INDIVIDUALS

Take an alphabet challenge. Choose 3 letters from the alphabet. Think of three vocabulary words for each letter. Then write the definition or draw an example for each word.

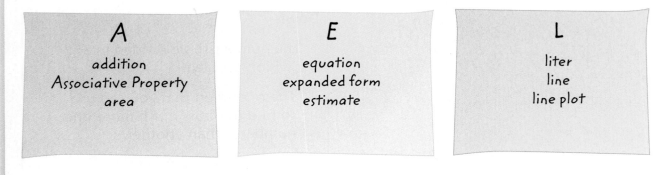

A	E	L
addition Associative Property area	equation expanded form estimate	liter line line plot

▶ Concentration PAIRS

Write the vocabulary words and related words from a unit on index cards. Write the definitions on a different set of index cards. Mix up both sets of cards. Then place the cards facedown on a table in an array, for example, 3 by 3 or 3 by 4. Take turns turning over two cards. If one card is a word and one card is a definition that matches the word, take the pair. Continue until each word has been matched with its definition.

area		
		The number of square units that cover a figure.

▶ Math Journal INDIVIDUALS

As you learn new words, write them in your Math Journal. Write the definition of the word and include a sketch or an example. As you learn new information about the word, add notes to your definition.

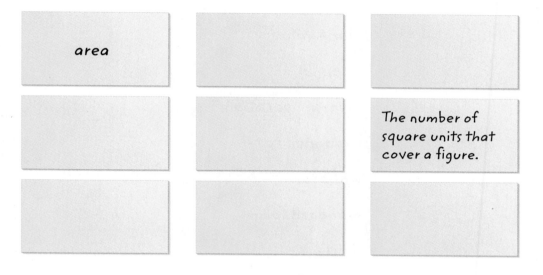

Angle: A figure formed by two rays with the same endpoint.

Degree: A unit for measuring angles.

Vocabulary Activities (continued)

▶ What's the Word? PAIRS

Work together to make a poster or bulletin board display of the words in a unit. Write definitions on a set of index cards. Mix up the cards. Work with a partner, choosing a definition from the index cards. Have your partner point to the word on the poster and name the matching math vocabulary word. Switch roles and try the activity again.

array

place value

addend

inverse operations

expanded form

word form

standard form

digit

one of two or more numbers added together to find a sum

Glossary

acute angle An angle smaller than a right angle.

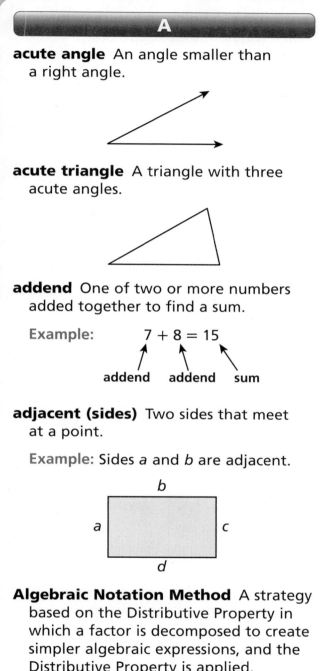

acute triangle A triangle with three acute angles.

addend One of two or more numbers added together to find a sum.

Example:

$$7 + 8 = 15$$

addend addend sum

adjacent (sides) Two sides that meet at a point.

Example: Sides *a* and *b* are adjacent.

Algebraic Notation Method A strategy based on the Distributive Property in which a factor is decomposed to create simpler algebraic expressions, and the Distributive Property is applied.

Example:
$$9 \cdot 28 = 9 \cdot (20 + 8)$$
$$= (9 \cdot 20) + (9 \cdot 8)$$
$$= 180 + 72$$
$$= 252$$

analog clock A clock with a face and hands.

angle A figure formed by two rays with the same endpoint.

area The number of square units that cover a figure.

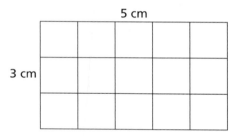

array An arrangement of objects, symbols, or numbers in rows and columns.

Associative Property of Addition Grouping the addends in different ways does not change the sum.

Example:
$$3 + (5 + 7) = 15$$
$$(3 + 5) + 7 = 15$$

Glossary (continued)

Associative Property of Multiplication
Grouping the factors in different ways does not change the product.

Example: $3 \times (5 \times 7) = 105$
$(3 \times 5) \times 7 = 105$

B

bar graph A graph that uses bars to show data. The bars may be vertical or horizontal.

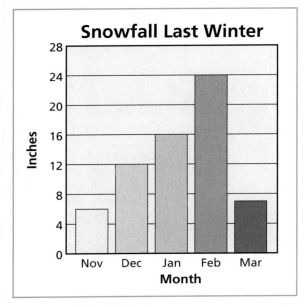

break-apart drawing A diagram that shows two addends and the sum.

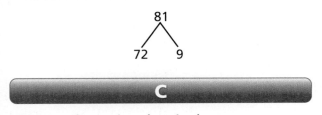

C

center The point that is the same distance from every point on the circle.

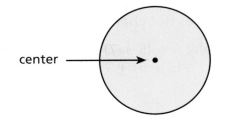

centimeter A unit of measure in the metric system that equals one hundredth of a meter. $100 \text{ cm} = 1 \text{ m}$

circle A plane figure that forms a closed path so that all the points on the path are the same distance from a point called the center.

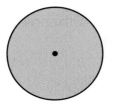

circle graph A graph that uses parts of a circle to show data.

Example:

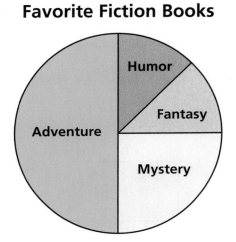

column A part of a table or array that contains items arranged vertically.

common denominator A common multiple of two or more denominators.

Example: A common denominator of $\frac{1}{2}$ and $\frac{1}{3}$ is 6 because 6 is a multiple of 2 and 3.

Commutative Property of Addition Changing the order of addends does not change the sum.

Example: $3 + 8 = 11$
$8 + 3 = 11$

Commutative Property of Multiplication Changing the order of factors does not change the product.

Example: $3 \times 8 = 24$
$8 \times 3 = 24$

compare Describe quantities as greater than, less than, or equal to each other.

comparison bars Bars that represent the larger amount and smaller amount in a comparison situation.

For addition and subtraction:

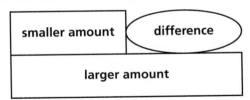

For multiplication and division:

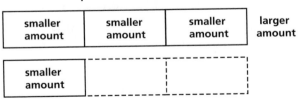

comparison situation A situation in which two amounts are compared by addition or by multiplication. An *addition comparison situation* compares by asking or telling how much more (how much less) one amount is than another. A *multiplication comparison situation* compares by asking or telling how many times as many one amount is as another. The multiplication comparison may also be made using fraction language. For example, you can say, "Sally has one fourth as much as Tom has," instead of saying "Tom has 4 times as much as Sally has."

composite number A number greater than 1 that has more than one factor pair. Examples of composite numbers are 10 and 18. The factor pairs of 10 are 1 and 10, 2 and 5. The factor pairs of 18 are 1 and 18, 2 and 9, 3 and 6.

cup A unit of liquid volume in the customary system that equals 8 fluid ounces.

D

data A collection of information.

decimal number A representation of a number using the numerals 0 to 9, in which each digit has a value 10 times the digit to its right. A dot or **decimal point** separates the whole-number part of the number on the left from the fractional part on the right.

Examples: 1.23 and 0.3

Glossary (continued)

decimal point A symbol used to separate dollars and cents in money amounts or to separate ones and tenths in decimal numbers.

Examples:

$8.59   1.2

↑   ↑

decimal point

decimeter A unit of measure in the metric system that equals one tenth of a meter. 10 dm = 1 m

degree (°) A unit for measuring angles.

denominator The number below the bar in a fraction. It shows the total number of equal parts in the fraction.

Example:

$\frac{3}{4}$ ← denominator

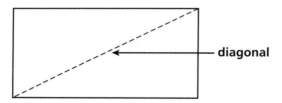

diagonal A line segment that connects vertices of a polygon, but is not a side of the polygon.

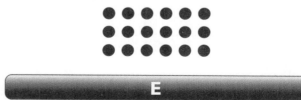

← diagonal

difference The result of a subtraction.

Example: 54 − 37 = 17 ← difference

digit Any of the symbols 0, 1, 2, 3, 4, 5, 6, 7, 8, or 9.

digital clock A clock that shows us the hour and minutes with numbers.

Digit-by-Digit A method used to solve a division problem.

Put in only one digit at a time.

$$7 \overline{)3{,}822}$$
$$-\ 3\ 5$$
$$\overline{32}$$
5

$$7 \overline{)3{,}822}$$
$$-\ 3\ 5$$
$$\overline{32}$$
$$-\ 28$$
$$\overline{42}$$
54

$$7 \overline{)3{,}822}$$
$$-\ 3\ 5$$
$$\overline{32}$$
$$-\ 28$$
$$\overline{42}$$
$$-\ 42$$
546

Distributive Property You can multiply a sum by a number, or multiply each addend by the number and add the products; the result is the same.

Example:

$3 \times (2 + 4) = (3 \times 2) + (3 \times 4)$

$3 \times 6 \quad = \quad 6 \ + \ 12$

$18 \quad = \quad 18$

dividend The number that is divided in division.

Example: $9\overline{)63}^{\,7}$ 63 is the dividend.

divisible A number is divisible by another number if the quotient is a whole number with a remainder of 0.

divisor The number you divide by in division.

Example: $9\overline{)63}^{\,7}$ 9 is the divisor.

dot array An arrangement of dots in rows and columns.

● ● ● ● ● ●
● ● ● ● ● ●
● ● ● ● ● ●

E

elapsed time The time that passes between the beginning and the end of an activity.

© Houghton Mifflin Harcourt Publishing Company

endpoint The point at either end of a line segment or the beginning point of a ray.

endpoint   endpoint   endpoint

equation A statement that two expressions are equal. It has an equal sign.

Examples: $32 + 35 = 67$
$67 = 32 + 34 + 1$
$(7 \times 8) + 1 = 57$

equilateral Having all sides of equal length.

Example: An equilateral triangle

equivalent fractions Two or more fractions that represent the same number.

Example: $\frac{2}{4}$ and $\frac{4}{8}$ are equivalent because they both represent one half.

estimate A number close to an exact amount or to find about how many or how much.

evaluate Substitute a value for a letter (or symbol) and then simplify the expression.

expanded form A way of writing a number that shows the value of each of its digits.

Example: Expanded form of 835:
$800 + 30 + 5$
8 hundreds + 3 tens + 5 ones

Expanded Notation A method used to solve multiplication and division problems.

Examples:

43 × 67

$$\begin{array}{r} 67 = 60 + 7 \\ \times\, 43 = 40 + 3 \\ \hline 40 \times 60 = 2400 \\ 40 \times 7\ =\ 280 \\ 3 \times 60\ =\ 180 \\ 3 \times 7\ =\ +\,21 \\ \hline 2{,}881 \end{array}$$

3,822 ÷ 7

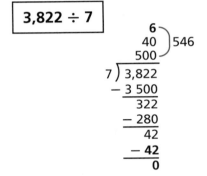

expression One or more numbers, variables, or numbers and variables with one or more operations.

Examples: 4
$6x$
$6x - 5$
$7 + 4$

F

factor One of two or more numbers multiplied to find a product.

Example:

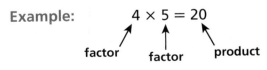

$4 \times 5 = 20$

factor   factor   product

© Houghton Mifflin Harcourt Publishing Company

Glossary (continued)

factor pair A factor pair for a number is a pair of whole numbers whose product is that number.

Example: $5 \times 7 = 35$

factor pair   product

fluid ounce A unit of liquid volume in the customary system.
8 fluid ounces = 1 cup

foot A U.S. customary unit of length equal to 12 inches.

formula An equation with letters or symbols that describes a rule.

The formula for the area of a rectangle is:

$A = l \times w$

where A is the area, l is the length, and w is the width.

fraction A number that is the sum of unit fractions, each an equal part of a set or part of a whole.

Examples: $\frac{3}{4} = \frac{1}{4} + \frac{1}{4} + \frac{1}{4}$

$\frac{5}{4} = \frac{1}{4} + \frac{1}{4} + \frac{1}{4} + \frac{1}{4} + \frac{1}{4}$

G

gallon A unit of liquid volume in the customary system that equals 4 quarts.

gram The basic unit of mass in the metric system.

greater than (>) A symbol used to compare two numbers. The greater number is given first below.

Example: $33 > 17$
33 is greater than 17.

group To combine numbers to form new tens, hundreds, thousands, and so on.

H

hundredth A unit fraction representing one of one hundred parts, written as 0.01 or $\frac{1}{100}$.

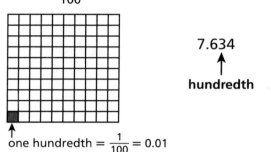

7.634
hundredth

one hundredth $= \frac{1}{100} = 0.01$

I

Identity Property of Multiplication The product of 1 and any number equals that number.

Example: $10 \times 1 = 10$

inch A U.S. customary unit of length.

Example: 1 inch

inequality A statement that two expressions are not equal.

Examples: $2 < 5$
$4 + 5 > 12 - 8$

inverse operations Opposite or reverse operations that undo each other. Addition and subtraction are inverse operations. Multiplication and division are inverse operations.

Examples: $4 + 6 = 10$ so, $10 - 6 = 4$
and $10 - 4 = 6$.
$3 \times 9 = 27$ so, $27 \div 9 = 3$
and $27 \div 3 = 9$.

isosceles triangle A triangle with at least two sides of equal length.

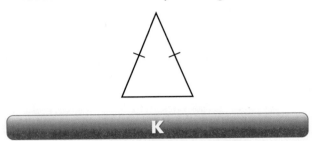

K

kilogram A unit of mass in the metric system that equals one thousand grams. 1 kg = 1,000 g

kiloliter A unit of liquid volume in the metric system that equals one thousand liters. 1 kL = 1,000 L

kilometer A unit of length in the metric system that equals 1,000 meters. 1 km = 1,000 m

L

least common denominator The least common multiple of two or more denominators.

Example: The least common denominator of $\frac{1}{2}$ and $\frac{1}{3}$ is 6 because 6 is the smallest multiple of 2 and 3.

length The measure of a line segment or one side of a figure.

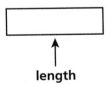

length

less than (<) A symbol used to compare two numbers. The smaller number is given first below.

Example: 54 < 78
54 is less than 78.

line A straight path that goes on forever in opposite directions.

Example: line *AB*

line of symmetry A line on which a figure can be folded so that the two halves match exactly.

— line of symmetry

line plot A diagram that shows the frequency of data on a number line. Also called a dot plot.

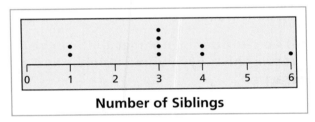

Number of Siblings

line segment Part of a line that has two endpoints.

line symmetry A figure has line symmetry if it can be folded along a line to create two halves that match exactly.

liquid volume A measure of the space a liquid occupies.

liter The basic unit of liquid volume in the metric system. 1 liter = 1,000 milliliters

© Houghton Mifflin Harcourt Publishing Company

Glossary (continued)

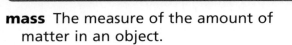
mass The measure of the amount of matter in an object.

meter The basic unit of length in the metric system.

metric system A base ten system of measurement.

mile A U.S. customary unit of length equal to 5,280 feet.

milligram A unit of mass in the metric system. 1,000 mg = 1g

milliliter A unit of liquid volume in the metric system. 1,000 mL = 1 L

millimeter A unit of length in the metric system. 1,000 mm = 1 m

mixed number A number that can be represented by a whole number and a fraction.

Example: $4\frac{1}{2} = 4 + \frac{1}{2}$

multiple A number that is the product of a given number and any whole number.

Examples:

4 × 1 = 4, so 4 is a multiple of 4.
4 × 2 = 8, so 8 is a multiple of 4.

N

number line A line that extends, without end, in each direction and shows numbers as a series of points. The location of each number is shown by its distance from 0.

numerator The number above the bar in a fraction. It shows the number of equal parts.

Example:

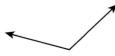

$\frac{3}{4}$ ⟵ numerator $\frac{3}{4} = \frac{1}{4} + \frac{1}{4} + \frac{1}{4}$

O

obtuse angle An angle greater than a right angle and less than a straight angle.

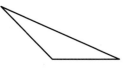

obtuse triangle A triangle with one obtuse angle.

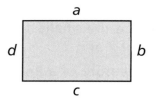

opposite sides Sides that are across from each other; they do not meet at a point.

Example: Sides *a* and *c* are opposite.

```
        a
   ┌─────────┐
 d │         │ b
   └─────────┘
        c
```

Order of Operations A set of rules that state the order in which operations should be done.

STEPS: -Compute inside parentheses first.

-Multiply and divide from left to right.

-Add and subtract from left to right.

ounce A unit of weight.
16 ounces = 1 pound
A unit of liquid volume (also called a fluid ounce).
8 ounces = 1 cup

P

parallel Lines in the same plane that never intersect are parallel. Line segments and rays that are part of parallel lines are also parallel.

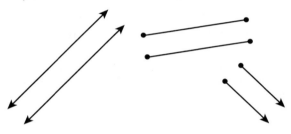

parallelogram A quadrilateral with both pairs of opposite sides parallel.

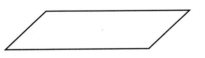

partial product The product of the ones, or tens, or hundreds, and so on in multidigit multiplication.

Example:

```
    24
  ×  9
  ————
    36   ←  partial product (9 × 4)
   180   ←  partial product (9 × 20)
  ————
   216
```

perimeter The distance around a figure.

perpendicular Lines, line segments, or rays are perpendicular if they form right angles.

Example: These two lines are perpendicular.

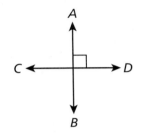

pictograph A graph that uses pictures or symbols to represent data.

Books Checked Out of Library	
Student	
Najee	📖 📖
Tariq	📖 📖 📖 📖 📖 📖
Celine	📖 📖 📖 📖 📖 📖 📖 📖
Jamarcus	📖 📖 📖
Brooke	📖 📖 📖 📖

📖 = 5 books

pint A customary unit of liquid volume that equals 16 fluid ounces.

place value The value assigned to the place that a digit occupies in a number.

Example: 235

The 2 is in the hundreds place, so its value is 200.

Glossary (continued)

place value drawing A drawing that represents a number. Thousands are represented by vertical rectangles, hundreds are represented by squares, tens are represented by vertical lines, and ones by small circles.

Example:

2,697

Place Value Sections A method using rectangle drawings to solve multiplication or division problems.

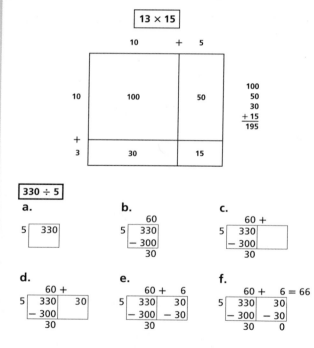

point A location in a plane. It is usually shown by a dot.

polygon A closed plane figure with sides made of straight line segments.

pound A unit of weight in the U.S. customary system.

prefix A letter or group of letters placed before a word to make a new word.

prime number A number greater than 1 that has 1 and itself as the only factor pair. Examples of prime numbers are 2, 7, and 13. The only factor pair of 7 is 1 and 7.

product The answer to a multiplication problem.

Example: $9 \times 7 = 63$

↑
product

protractor A semicircular tool for measuring and constructing angles.

Q

quadrilateral A polygon with four sides.

quart A customary unit of liquid volume that equals 32 ounces or 4 cups.

quotient The answer to a division problem.

Example: $9\overline{)63}$ with 7 above — 7 is the quotient.

R

ray Part of a line that has one endpoint and extends without end in one direction.

rectangle A parallelogram with four right angles.

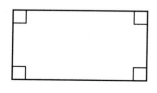

© Houghton Mifflin Harcourt Publishing Company

reflex angle An angle with a measure that is greater than 180° and less than 360°.

remainder The number left over after dividing two numbers that are not evenly divisible.

Example:  The remainder is 3.

rhombus A parallelogram with sides of equal length.

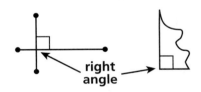

right angle One of four angles made by perpendicular line segments.

right triangle A triangle with one right angle.

round To find the nearest ten, hundred, thousand, or some other place value. The usual rounding rule is to round up if the next digit to the right is 5 or more and round down if the next digit to the right is less than 5.

Examples: 463 rounded to the nearest ten is 460.
463 rounded to the nearest hundred is 500.

row A part of a table or array that contains items arranged horizontally.

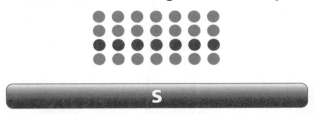

S

scalene A triangle with no equal sides is a scalene triangle.

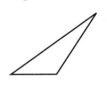

Shortcut Method A strategy for multiplying. It is the current common method in the United States.

Step 1	Step 2
$\overset{7}{2}8$	$\overset{7}{2}8$
$\times\ 9$	$\times\ 9$
2	252

simplest form A fraction is in simplest form if there is no whole number (other than 1) that divides evenly into the numerator and denominator.

Example: $\frac{3}{4}$ This fraction is in simplest form because no number divides evenly into 3 and 4.

simplify an expression Combine like terms and perform operations until all terms have been combined.

simplify a fraction To divide the numerator and the denominator of a fraction by the same number to make an equivalent fraction made from fewer but larger unit fractions.

Example: $\frac{5}{10} = \frac{5 \div 5}{10 \div 5} = \frac{1}{2}$

Glossary (continued)

situation equation An equation that shows the structure of the information in a problem.

Example: $35 + n = 40$

solution equation An equation that shows the operation that can be used to solve the problem.

Example: $n = 40 - 35$

square A rectangle with 4 sides of equal length and 4 right angles. It is also a rhombus.

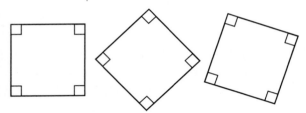

square array An array in which the number of rows equals the number of columns.

square centimeter A unit of area equal to the area of a square with one-centimeter sides.

square decimeter A unit of area equal to the area of a square with one-decimeter sides.

square foot A unit of area equal to the area of a square with one-foot sides.

square inch A unit of area equal to the area of a square with one-inch sides.

square kilometer A unit of area equal to the area of a square with one-kilometer sides.

square meter A unit of area equal to the area of a square with one-meter sides.

square mile A unit of area equal to the area of a square with one-mile sides.

square millimeter A unit of area equal to the area of a square with one-millimeter sides.

square unit A unit of area equal to the area of a square with one-unit sides.

square yard A unit of area equal to the area of a square with one-yard sides.

standard form The form of a number written using digits.

Example: 2,145

straight angle An angle that measures 180°.

sum The answer when adding two or more addends.

Example:

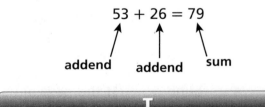

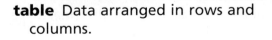

table Data arranged in rows and columns.

tenth A unit fraction representing one of ten equal parts of a whole, written as 0.1 or $\frac{1}{10}$.

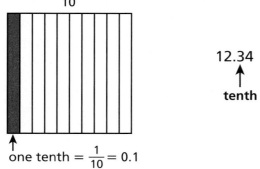

12.34
↑
tenth

one tenth $= \frac{1}{10} = 0.1$

term in an expression A number, variable, product, or quotient in an expression. Each term is separated by an operation sign $(+, -)$.

Example: $3n + 5$ has two terms, $3n$ and 5.

thousandth A unit fraction representing one of one thousand equal parts of a whole, written as 0.001 or $\frac{1}{1,000}$.

ton A unit of weight that equals 2,000 pounds.

tonne A metric unit of mass that equals 1,000 kilograms.

total Sum. The result of addition.

Example: $53 + 26 = 79$

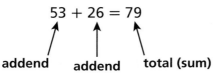

addend   addend   total (sum)

trapezoid A quadrilateral with exactly one pair of parallel sides.

triangle A polygon with three sides.

unit A standard of measurement.

Examples: Centimeters, pounds, inches, and so on.

unit fraction A fraction whose numerator is 1. It shows one equal part of a whole.

Example: $\frac{1}{4}$

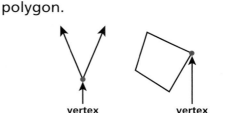

variable A letter or a symbol that represents a number in an algebraic expression.

vertex A point that is shared by two sides of an angle or two sides of a polygon.

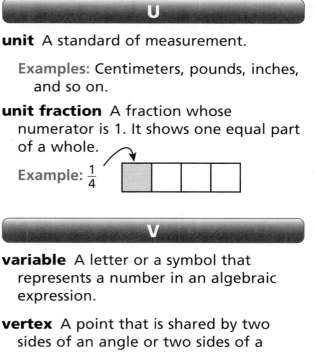

vertex   vertex

width The measure of one side of a figure.

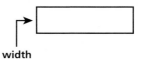

width

word form The form of a number written using words instead of digits.

Example: Six hundred thirty-nine

yard A U.S. customary unit of length equal to 3 feet.

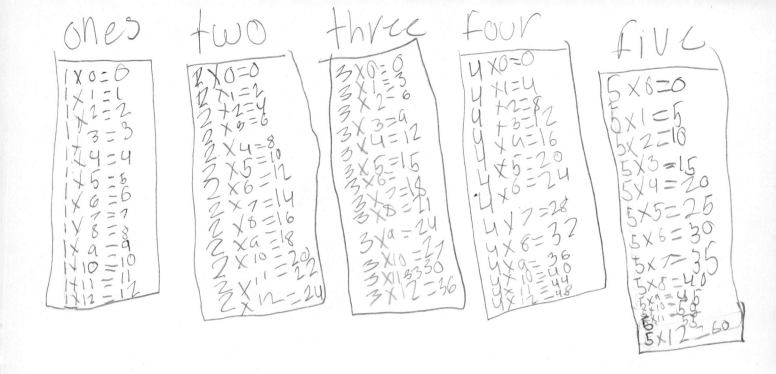

ones	two	three	four	five
1 × 0 = 0	2 × 0 = 0	3 × 0 = 0	4 × 0 = 0	5 × 0 = 0
1 × 1 = 1	2 × 1 = 2	3 × 1 = 3	4 × 1 = 4	5 × 1 = 5
1 × 2 = 2	2 × 2 = 4	3 × 2 = 6	4 × 2 = 8	5 × 2 = 10
1 × 3 = 3	2 × 3 = 6	3 × 3 = 9	4 × 3 = 12	5 × 3 = 15
1 × 4 = 4	2 × 4 = 8	3 × 4 = 12	4 × 4 = 16	5 × 4 = 20
1 × 5 = 5	2 × 5 = 10	3 × 5 = 15	4 × 5 = 20	5 × 5 = 25
1 × 6 = 6	2 × 6 = 12	3 × 6 = 18	4 × 6 = 24	5 × 6 = 30
1 × 7 = 7	2 × 7 = 14	3 × 7 = 18	4 × 7 = 28	5 × 7 = 35
1 × 8 = 8	2 × 8 = 16	3 × 8 = 21	4 × 8 = 32	5 × 8 = 40
1 × 9 = 9	2 × 9 = 18	3 × 9 = 24	4 × 9 = 36	5 × 9 = 45
1 × 10 = 10	2 × 10 = 20	3 × 10 = 27	4 × 10 = 40	5 × 10 = 50
1 × 11 = 11	2 × 11 = 22	3 × 11 = 30	4 × 11 = 44	5 × 11 = 55
1 × 12 = 12	2 × 12 = 24	3 × 12 = 36	4 × 12 = 48	5 × 12 = 60